Practical Essay Writing

Kristine Brown

Viva Books

New Delhi | Mumbai | Chennai | Kolkata | Bengaluru | Hyderabad | Kochi | Guwahati

First Indian Edition 2012

VIVA BOOKS PRIVATE LIMITED

- 4737/23 Ansari Road, Daryaganj, New Delhi 110 002
- E-mail: vivadelhi@vivagroupindia.net, Tel. 42242200
- 76, Service Industries, Shirvane, Sector 1, Nerul, Navi Mumbai 400 706
  E-mail: vivamumbai@vivagroupindia.net, Tel. 27721273, 27721274
- Jamals Fazal Chambers, 26 Greams Road, Chennai 600 006
  E-mail: vivachennai@vivagroupindia.net, Tel. 28290304, 28294241
- B-103, Jindal Towers, 21/1A/3 Darga Road, Kolkata 700 017
  E-mail: vivakolkata@vivagroupindia.net, Tel. 22836381, 22816713
- 7, Sovereign Park Apartments, 56-58, K. R. Road, Basavanagudi, Bengaluru 560 004
  E-mail: vivabangalore@vivagroupindia.net, Tel. 26607409, 26607410
- 101-102 Mughal Marc Apartments, 3-4-637 to 641, Narayanguda, Hyderabad 500 029
  E-mail: vivahyderabad@vivagroupindia.net, Tel. 27564481, 27564482
- First Floor, Beevi Towers, SRM Road, Kaloor, Kochi 682 018, Kerala
  E-mail: vivakochi@vivagroupindia.net, Tel: 0484-2403055, 2403056
- 232, GNB Road, Beside UCO Bank, Silpukhuri, Guwahati 781 003
  E-mail: vivaguwahati@vivagroupindia.net, Tel: 0361-2666386

www.vivagroupindia.com

Published by arrangement with
Pascal Educational Services
655 Parramatta Road
Leichhardt NSW 2040
Australia

ISBN: 978-81-309-1878-5

Published by Vinod Vasishtha for Viva Books Private Limited, 4737/23, Ansari Road, Daryaganj, New Delhi-110 002. Printed and bound by Anand Sons, Delhi - 110 092.

Acknowledgements

I would like to thank Jane Cafarella, of What-a-Cheek Enterprises, for the cartoons used throughout the book.

I would also like to thank the following people for their kind permission to use materials:

- For essays (pages 95–97): Sam Tompkins, Hamish McLean and Hana Marjanac.
- For assorted paragraphs and for ideas on essay writing: Alli Barnard, Jacqui English, Penny Cleary, Matilda Brown, John Maloney, Rosie Brown, Hannah McLean, Kasey Tompkins, Amanda Spratt, Charlotte Boyer and Elizabeth Boyer.
- For *The Simpsons* essay question: Mrs Dwyer, Daramalan College, Dickson, ACT.
- For use of headlines and articles in collage (page 5): *The Blue Mountains Gazette* ('Residents remove graffiti', 'Aerosol art workshop', '$15,000 to help beat graffiti' and 'Facing Prejudice'); and Wayne Simpson, 'Facing Prejudice' letter to the editor.
- For use of headlines in collages (page 5, 21, 22): *The Sydney Morning Herald* ('Rock art or vandalism, Manly doesn't want it', 'Look up commuters, it's $500 if you bag a tagger', 'Councils target graffiti on private land', 'Graffiti goes bye-bye', 'Books; Facing their final chapter?', 'Britannica unbound as books abandoned', 'Books are bound to change', 'Deal at last over stolen mobiles bar', 'Love in the time of mobiles' and 'iv jst gt 2 get a msg 2U').
- For use of articles in collages (page 5, 21, 22): Scott Rochfort, 'Look up commuters, it's $500 if you bag a tagger'; Juan-Carlo Tomas and Nadia Jamal, 'Rock art or vandalism, Manly doesn't want it'; Anne Davies, 'Councils target graffiti on private land'; Sue Lowe, 'Deal at last over stolen mobiles ban'; Lauren Martin, 'Love in the time of mobiles' and 'iv jst gt 2 get a msg 2U'.
- For photographs used in collage: Edwina Pickles (page 5).
- For use of articles and article extracts: Miranda Wood, 'Certificate students lost for words' (page 19); Daniel Tucker, 'Graffiti: Art and Crime' (pages 55, 56); Doug Johnson and Linworth Publishing, Inc., 'The Future of Books' (pages 26, 27); Mark Butler, 'You got the book' (pages 71, 94); Xia Lin and John Hubbard, 'Books of the future' (page 77); Sue Lowe, 'Brave New World' (page 91); Martin Lindstrom, 'Message Madness our big chance' (page 91); Jack Waterford and The Canberra Times, 'Upwardly mobile on easy street' (page 91); Charles Wright, 'O grammar where art thou' (page 91); Lauren Martin, 'Love in the time of mobiles' (page 91); Andy Lamey and the National Post, 'Simpsons revealed as models of family values' (pages 92–93); Ray Archee, 'The last word' (page 93); Douglas Rushkoff, 'People, not computers, kill books' (page 93); Keith Austin, 'Sign of the tomes' (page 94); Malcolm Knox, 'The book is dead, long live the book' (page 94).
- For use of the cartoon about mobile phones: Phil Somerville (page 92).

Kristine Brown

Before you start

While writing this book, I asked some students to define the word 'essay'. This was the response from one Year 10 student:

> *An essay is a piece of writing that some idiot invented just to destroy teenagers' TV viewing time. Teachers hand out these things called 'essays' just to ensure their students have no 'life factor'. Essays suck!*

Strong words! But let's face it, many of you probably feel the same way. Essays have a bad reputation. For many school students, the very idea of writing an essay fills them with fear and anxiety, a rather unpleasant feeling in the pit of the stomach and the urgent need to do other really important things ... like thoroughly clearing the desk, sharpening every pencil within sight, going to the shops to buy some better writing paper, and – when things are really desperate – helping out your parents with the housework.

Well, I want to share five secrets that might make you feel better about essays.

1 Essays don't deserve their bad reputation. Essays are easy. Let me correct that. Like anything else in life, they are easy **when you know how**.

2 You already have many writing skills and experiences that are useful for essay writing. Essays **are** different from, say, stories, descriptions or reports, but the skills you use are the same. You are just applying them in a different way.

3 It **is** possible to learn how to write good essays.

4 Essays are used in many school subjects – not only in English. You can't avoid them, so it is a good idea to learn how to write them.

5 If you learn how to write essays in your junior secondary years, you will have a head start in senior secondary school.

So, **Essay Writing Step-by-Step** aims to make essays easy for you by showing you the 'how' of essay writing. It sets out five basic steps to writing a good essay:

Step 1: Understand about essays
Step 2: Prepare to write
Step 3: Make a first draft
Step 4: Revise and polish
Step 5: Do a final check

Each step offers you a number of Tasks pages to help you practise the skills you'll need. Answers are given at the back of the book, and the page references for the answers are given at the top of each Tasks page (eg. A PAGE 99).

Essay Writing Step-by-Step uses one main essay as a model throughout but, from Step 2 onwards, helps you to work through ideas for three quite different essay questions. From Step 3 onwards you choose one of these questions to take to the drafting, revising and final check stages.

I hope you feel better about essays after using this book, and that next time you have to tackle one you feel you can sit down and start working on it right away – without taking a trip to the shops or feeling the need to do housework. **Good luck!**

CONTENTS

STEP ONE 1

Understand about essays

You can't really write a good essay without understanding some important things about writing, and about writing essays in particular.

In this Step we will use one essay as a model to demonstrate some of the basic things you need to understand about essays:

1. What exactly is an essay?
2. Why do we write essays?
3. How is an essay different from speech and other writing?
4. Are all essays the same?
5. What is the basic essay structure?

The Model Essay we will use is on the question:

Graffiti should be seen as a form of art. Do you agree or disagree?

The aim of this section is really to raise your awareness of some important points. All of these points come up again later in the book where they are treated in more detail.

1 What exactly is an essay?

Some student ideas

As already mentioned, I asked a few students the important question "What is an essay?" Here are their answers:

> *I don't really know ... um ... a piece of writing on a topic? (Year 7)*
> *A longer written response to a question or a statement. (Year 8)*
> *A kind of extended response on a question and you expand the ideas and try to discuss it and relate it to current events. You can put your own opinions into it. (Year 9)*
> *A structured piece of writing about a given statement, presenting arguments and not writing in the first person ('I') (Year 9)*
> *An essay is a piece of writing organised into three parts – introducing, exploring and concluding on a topic in an orderly fashion. (Year 9)*
> *Basically it is supporting a point, giving your ideas on the point and on nothing else. (Year 10)*
> *Gathering information to answer a question, including quotes, and then writing it in a set format – Introduction, Body and Conclusion. (Year 10)*

Taken together, these students covered some very important points about essays:

- they are longish pieces of writing
- they are on a set topic or question
- they are structured – an Introduction, Body and Conclusion
- they include facts and information
- they include your own opinions
- they are formal
- they are not personal
- they support one point all the way through
- they do not include information on anything besides the one point.

A basic definition

If we pull their ideas together into a basic definition, we get something like this:

> ***An essay is a formal,*** ① ***structured piece of writing which makes a statement on a topic*** ② ***or question, and which supports*** ③ ***this statement throughout with information and ideas.***

Let's break up this definition and have a look at it.

An essay is a formal, structured piece of writing ... ①

This covers two important things. Firstly, essays are formal. The best way to understand what 'formal' means is to think that it is the absolute and complete opposite of the way you might talk with your very best friend. It is not personal, friendly and casual. It is reserved, distant and quite serious.

Secondly, essays are structured. Essays are quite long pieces of writing. For this reason alone, it is important that you structure your writing in the way that will best help your reader to follow you and in a way that he or she expects you to. Put very simply, you tell your reader what you are going to write about (the Introduction), then you write about it (the Body) and then you tell your reader what you have written (the Conclusion).

**

... which makes a statement on a topic or question ... ②

This simply means that you say something directly about the essay question. What you say depends very much on the essay topic and the type of essay. In most cases it will be a statement of your point of view on the essay question, but this is not always true. In some types of essays, for example, it might be simply a restatement of the essay question. Whatever it is, it is **hugely** important. It:

- is the short, direct response to the essay question
- states one clear idea
- is generally one sentence only
- ties your whole essay together
- comes in the first paragraph (the Introduction).

If you don't have a statement like this, you don't have an essay. It is where you say to your reader:
Look, I am saying this to you about this essay topic.

**

... and which supports this statement throughout with information and ideas. ③

Of course it is not enough to simply say to your reader: *I am saying this to you*. You have to expand on this statement – you have to prove it, or explain it, or discuss it, or in some way say more about it. You have to go on to say, for example:

... I believe this because X, Y and Z

or
... I can explain this in this way – X, Y and Z
or
... here are some of the important issues related to this – X, Y, Z.

This is what the main section of your essay does. It supports and develops the statement on the essay question at the beginning of your essay.

**

So, there are four important things to remember about all this:

- You **must** have one idea which holds your whole essay together from start to finish.
- You **must** make a statement about this idea at the beginning of your essay.
- You should **not** just write everything you know on the topic. Instead, you should choose information and ideas which help you develop your statement.
- You **must** organise or structure the whole essay so that the reader can make sense of it.

Tasks

PAGE 99
(answer page)

1 Read the Model Essay question on the next page and look at the newspaper collage. Then read the Model Essay on page 6.
Does the writer:

- completely agree with the view in the essay question? ______
- completely disagree with the view in the essay question? ______
- partly agree and partly disagree? ______

In which sentence in the first paragraph (the Introduction) does the writer make a statement about this view? ______

What points does the writer make to support this statement? ______

______

______

______

Can you see clearly where and how the writer:

- tells you what she is going to write about ______
- writes about it ______
- tells you what she has written about? ______

2 Look at these Introduction paragraphs on the same essay question. In each one, underline the main statement of view on the essay question. *Hint*: Look for the clearest and most direct statement relating to the question.

a Street art has been around for a very long time. People were painting on cave walls thousands of years ago. Graffiti is simply a modern version of this ancient artistic tradition. It is only because it is on the street and not in an art gallery that people are so negative towards it.

b Many of the streets in our cities have been destroyed in recent years by graffiti. Graffiti is nothing more than vandalism and should never be considered as a form of art. The costs to the individuals and to the community in general are enormous.

c Graffiti is a new form of art and should be made legal. However, this is unlikely to happen because of prejudice in our community against youth and their interests and activities.

d Graffiti has become a very big problem in our cities and towns. Huge amounts of public money are being spent cleaning it up. There is no way that this destructive activity should ever be considered as art. It is generally very ugly and usually done simply to irritate the authorities and members of the public.

3 These two paragraphs were in an early draft of this essay. Why do you think the writer decided to leave them out?

a Youth are treated differently to adults in all sorts of ways. For example, young people standing around shopping centres can be asked to move on but older people cannot. Young people are more likely to be fined rather than warned for not having tickets on public transport. If an adult is caught holding a spray can, nothing is likely to happen but if a teen or young adult is caught, he or she is fined and arrested.

b My brother did a spray can art work based on a Picasso painting for his Higher School Certificate. He won a prize for it and somebody even bought it, so it shows that some people recognise graffiti as art. The person who bought it now has it hanging in his living room. Really art is all in the eye of the beholder.

Graffiti should be seen as a form of art. Do you agree or disagree?

LETTERS

Facing prejudice

I am writing to express my views on the graffiti "issue" that has been the topic of a great deal of heated discussion in the Gazette in the last few months.

I am amazed by some of the letters published in the Gazette in recent times written by people who regard themselves as art critics of some kind. One so-called "art critic" went so far as to compare graffiti vandals to his dog, which seems to have some kind of bladder control problem (not mentioning any names). There is yet another "art critic" who considers himself such an expert on all things graffiti that he has b... dubbed "Mr. Graffiti".

Yet I doubt these two gen... capable to operate a ca... skill and accurac... from the P...

general public usually only see these "tags" they are led to believe that this is all graffiti is, however tags are only a small part of a much more diverse art form. Perhaps if local businesses and the council work with the writers, we can work out a plan which will lessen these "tags" and bring the real art of graffiti into the forefront. Thereby educating these "art critic..." and ending this debate.

Springwood. — WA...

...ing a tagger

Look up, commuters, it's $500

Scott Rochfort

Don't be surprised if there are more watchful eyes on the train this morning.

Passengers are being offered $500 for information leading to the conviction of graffiti artists and vandals during Operation Tag, a six-week campaign launched yesterday by State Rail and police.

...Rail spends more than ...on remov-ing graffiti and associated work. CityRail says that more than 3000 of its Sydney rail carriages are sprayed with graffiti every month, with attacks expected to increase during school holidays.

The chief executive of State Rail, Howard Lacy, said people should report graffiti immediately so vandals could be caught in the act.

Mr Lacy said State Rail wanted to target 130 offenders "identified" in the past 18 months.

"Many people will try and t... you that graffiti is a legitim... form of social expression. ...don't agree," he said.

Aesthetics aside, Mr Lac... the blitz was aimed at st... unsafe behaviour by vand... the past 18 months, nine have either being killed ...iously injured in NS... vandalising trains.

There were also "gangs" fiddling wit... an attempt to stop tr...

Rock art or vandalism, Manly doesn't want it

Juan-Carlo Tomas and Nadia Jamal

Children thought it was the Wiggles' Dorothy the Dinosaur, a tourist asked if it was Aboriginal and locals wondered if it was sculpture by the sea.

But no-one – not Manly Council, residents or police – could say for sure yesterday who did it, why they did it or what it was.

Sydneysiders have until lunchtime today to make up their own mind about our latest paint job: a large rock at Shelly Beach daubed in aqua blue with white polka dots.

What authorities do know is that early on Saturday someone – or a group – lugged quite a bit of paint and equipment around the headland to get to it.

Late yesterday, council workers started to blast water at high-pressure to remove what is believed to be acrylic household paint. A special net has been suspended under the rock to stop paint particles getting into the water. The cost to ratepayers: $1000.

The Mayor of Manly, Jean Hay, said she was "absolutely devastated".

"The people who are involved in this deliberate act of vandalism should absolutely hang their heads in shame," she said..

"They are obviously brain dead to perform such a terrible act. It's quiet obvious that whoever has been involved, that they are professionals."

Council rangers interviewed nearby residents yesterday, and police said those responsible could be charged.

But opinion on the beach about the new look was divided. Some said it took away from the area's natural beauty, while others said it was fun.

"It's a beautiful place here, and it's spoiled it," said Greg Scott, 49, a former resident who now lives in London and is on holiday with his nephew Morgan Faets.

"I thought it may have been a marketing campaign, but someone would have claimed responsibility for it by now."

But Morgan, 13, had another hypothesis: "It's Dorothy the Dinosaur."

A Japanese tourist, looking up from the water, asked if it was Aboriginal before continuing on his swim.

Residents paint over the graffiti earlier this month. — Photo courtesy Steve Bennetts.

Residents remove graffiti

After running a story on the problems of graffiti ...n the front page of the local quarterly ...ewspaper "The 20 Mile Hollow", the editor of ...e Hollow and local railway station manager ...ris Parr, was astounded to receive a high level ...of feedback from the residents of Woodford. Chris put it to the residents of Woodford to conduct a clean up of more than 56 "graffiti tags" in and around the Appian Way rail bridge. The area includes the bridge over the GWH, the ramp to the bridge and associated signs that are a constant target for vandals.

After many requests to the council, government bodies and utilities in order to repair and clean the area and its structures, only the BMCC came to help with the cleaning of the local bus shelters of graffiti. The area involved is the gateway to the south and north-east of Woodford leading west off the highway.

With paint donated by CityRail to complete the task, 48 residents turned up with paintbrushes, rollers and paint pots in hand on a still smoky Sunday morning on January 6.

...ving already received more than a dozen ...e calls from residents who were apologetic ...t they were unable to make it through prior ...itments, Chris was still hard pressed to ...nough work for locals to do and within 30 ...s all of the tags within the area were ...out.

...ents then weeded and swept the roadside, ...nd removed fallen trees in a gesture for ...CC to not only conduct some roadside ...nce but to landscape the area.

...an 60 locals who have now submitted ...act details for future "paint outs" have ...also place larger amounts of pressure ...epartment to clean up their respective ...around Woodford.

$15,000 grant to help beat graffiti

Blue Mountains City Council has been awarded a $15,000 grant for a colourful project to help combat graffiti in Springwood.

Attorney General and Blue Mountains MP Bob Debus said the council funding was one of 56 grants made under the third round of the Carr Government's three-year Beat Graffiti scheme, as part of its innovative Graffiti Solutions program.

Blue Mountains City Council will use its grant to promote community artwork from young people around the Springwood commuter car park at Springwood.

The project will involve 'at risk' youths, who will prepare and paint aerosol murals, which will have a local and transport theme.

"I am sure the community will welcome this council initiative, which will be a valuable way to connect with local young people who may be at risk of becoming involved in anti-social activity, at the same time as tackling a significant graffiti problem," Mr Debus said.

Blue Mountains mayor Jim Angel said the project in Springwood would make a significant impact on the levels of vandalism in the area surrounding the car park.

"We have found that art projects inhibit the levels of graffiti, particularly in areas where the young people of the community have direct involvement in the artwork," Clr Angel said. "The whole community will benefit from this project."

...n private land

Writing on the wall . . . perpetrators call it art but councils say graffiti is unsightly. Photo: Edwina Pickles

...other major ... Angeles, Chicago, Seattle, ...rtland and Oklahoma ...," the Minister for Local ...ernment, Harry Woods, yesterday.

...raffiti costs the commu-...p to $100 million a year. ...perience and research ...proven that the most ...ve way to frustrate of-...s is to remove graffiti ...kly as possible and ...ep removing it when it re-appears."

Under laws introduced last year, councils can enter into voluntary agreements with land owners to remove unsightly graffiti.

Several councils, including Auburn, Blacktown, the City...

owners who... prone to graf... But Mr V... councils ne... power to be... graffiti and... tied up wit... The Lord... Frank Sar... new laws... "This h... issue for... Cr Sarto... is that r...

...walls are sought to involve the private ...ctor but only about 10 per ...property

he said from Darwin, where he and a team were working on a commission.

Mr Peet admitted he started ...career by illegally...

Graffiti goes bye-bye

Paint manufacturer Wattyl Australia says it has developed the world's first anti-graffiti paint. The company's Queensland branch says the clear lacquer, made of a unique silicon base, can be applied to concrete, brick work, wood and most painted surfaces, and that vandalism from most marker pens and aerosol paints can be removed using a high-pressure water hose.

Aerosol art workshop

THREE aerosol art workshops for young people will be held at the Winmalee Youth Centre during the second week of the school holidays.

They will run from April 22 to April 24 inclusive from 12pm to 4pm.

The workshops will take the youth through design principles and techniques and give them the opportunity to produce work for the youth Art Expo later in the year at the Braemer Gallery, Blue Mountains Mayor Jim Angel said.

"As part of the Springwood car park project, the existing ad hoc graffiti will be removed and replaced with locally themed murals.

"The murals will be in the pedestrian access ways and stairwells and the car par facade panels.

"We want to demonstrate to young people that the opportunity exists for them to legally express their art work in partnership with the rest of the community to enhance the landscape," the mayor said.

He said the car park project would build on the expertise developed from the implementation of the Lawson tunnel project which involved 20 young people, council, the RTA and CityRail.

"These community projects compliment the State Government's anti-graffiti package," he said.

Graffiti should be seen as a form of art. Do you agree or disagree?

Almost every week there is an article or letter in the newspaper on the subject of graffiti. Usually, the writers are complaining about quick and careless scrawls done on public or private property. This form of graffiti should not be considered as art, but other more complex and skilful forms should be. More advanced forms of graffiti brighten up our suburbs. These forms take great artistic skill to design and carry out. If they were recognised as art, young artists would have better opportunities to develop their skills and this would benefit the community.

It is important, first of all, to distinguish between three different types of graffiti. First, there is the 'tag' which is the stylised writing of the graffiti artist's name. Then, there is the 'throw-up' which is bigger and more time-consuming than the tag, but generally just big bubble letters in two colours. Lastly, there is the 'piece' (short for 'masterpiece') which takes considerable skill and time to execute. (Tucker, online, p. 3) Unfortunately most of what we see in our streets are tags and throw-ups and really just vandalism. They are generally done quickly and carelessly by people who do not think of themselves as artists. Pieces, on the other hand, are usually done by people who do see their work as art and themselves as artists.

If good graffiti is seen as art and then encouraged, it has the potential to improve the look of our streets and our transport systems. Good graffiti pieces are colourful, vibrant, and attractive. In most cases, they are far more attractive than the walls they are painted on, which in the old parts of cities are often ugly, dull and uncared for. There are many examples of spectacular murals in the inner city. In fact, some have even become tourist attractions. There are also excellent examples of graffiti on passenger or freight trains. However, because graffiti is usually seen as vandalism, no matter what the works look like they are usually painted over in dull colours (Tucker, online p. 5).

Real graffiti pieces require high level artistic skill to design and carry out. Pieces are usually designed to cover very large areas such as walls, and so have to be planned in detail on paper first. The designs are usually intricate and involve many colours. They are usually done with spray cans and large textas, but some artists use paint rollers as well. Many pieces are just as good as what you can see hanging in art galleries, but because they are on the street and mostly done by young people, they are not considered as art.

Recognising talented graffitists as artists would give them the opportunity to further develop their skills. Graffiti artists need spaces where they can develop their spray can skills without breaking the law. In some parts of the city, there are legal walls and spaces, but in others there are very few or none at all. Most of the best examples of graffiti art can be found on walls where the artists have been given permission to do their work by councils or other organisations. This means they have the time to polish their work to a high artistic standard. If this happened more, the whole community would benefit.

To sum up, there is more than one kind of graffiti. The more basic forms are generally not art. However, the more complex examples of graffiti are a form of art requiring considerable artistic skill. If these forms of graffiti were recognised as art, they could make our streets more attractive and, at the same time, give talented young artists an opportunity to develop their skills further and contribute their creative skills to their community.

Bibliography:

Chalfont, H. and Prigoff, J. (1987) *Spraycan Art*. Thames and Hudson, London.
Tucker, D.O., (no date) *Graffiti: Art and Crime* (*online*) http://www-atdp-berkeley.edu/Studentpages/cflores/historygraffiti.html

2 Why do we write essays?

Let's now look at another tough question: Why do we write essays?

There are three answers to this question. All are important.

Your teacher's purpose

Most of the students I talked to said "We write essays because our teachers tell us to". So here's another question. Why do teachers set essays?

Put simply, teachers set essays to find out what you think on a topic and to find out how much you know. But more than this, they want to see if you can use what you know to support and develop your ideas on the topic.

What does this mean for you? Well, it means that you write essays to show your teacher:

- what you think about a topic (your ideas and opinions)
- what you know about the topic (facts and other people's opinions)
- that you can use what you know to support and develop your ideas and opinions.

Clearly, then, your essay will usually be a combination of facts and opinions used in a way that meets your teacher's purpose in setting the essay.

Your overall purpose

OK, but there is something more to think about. What are you actually trying to achieve with your reader? What is your goal? You are not trying to entertain the reader, as you might in a story. You are not trying to inform your reader about something he or she does not know.

So what are you doing? Well, you are trying to **convince** them. Your overall purpose or goal is to convince your reader (usually your teacher) that what you are saying is right or at least a reasonable point of view. You are basically saying something like:

This is the way I see it.
and you want your reader to say
Yes, I see what you mean. In general, I agree with you.
This overall goal to convince your reader will affect **what** you write about and **how** you write it.

Your specific purpose

Now, as well as wanting to convince your reader, you will have a more specific purpose which will be determined by the essay question. In most cases your purpose will be to argue a case, to discuss an issue, or to explain something. We will look at this more specific purpose in the Step 2 sections on *Understanding the essay question* and *Organising the content*.

If you want your essays to be successful you will need to write with these **three** kinds of purposes in mind. This is not as hard as it sounds, I promise!

Tasks

PAGE 99

1 When writing essays, it is important to understand the difference between fact and opinion. Factual statements are statements that can be proved (or disproved) by observation or experience. Statements of opinion may sound factual, but if they cannot be proven they are only opinion.

Say whether the following statements are statements of fact (F) or statements of opinion (O). Give your reasons on another piece of paper.

- **a** The story was very sad. ______
- **b** The estimated population of Australia in 2000 was 19.2 million. ______
- **c** The tale of *Animal Farm* is an analogy for the Russian Revolution. ______
- **d** Nobody should have to wear school uniforms. ______
- **e** More and more people will move to live in cities over the next fifty years. ______
- **f** The hole in the ozone layer is mainly caused by chlorofluorocarbons. ______
- **g** Australians are getting fatter. ______
- **h** The society of Ancient Egypt was a highly religious one. ______

2 Decide which of the statements below are statements of opinion (O) and which are statements of fact (F). Then, in the columns below match each statement of opinion to a statement of fact that would help to make it a more convincing opinion.

- **a** A study found that computer games do not stimulate a vital part of the brain. ______
- **b** In the future, people will be able to artificially boost their intelligence. ______
- **c** Movies are sending out a message to young people that smoking is fun. ______
- **d** Scientists have already successfully injected mice with an extra 'smart' gene. ______
- **e** Studies of group behaviour have shown that if people cannot see the other person's eyes, communication can be misinterpreted. ______
- **f** Long periods of playing computer games are bad for children's intelligence. ______
- **g** E-mail is a risky form of communication. ______
- **h** 57% of leading characters in 1990's films smoked, compared with 14% of people of similar social backgrounds in the general population. ______

Statements of opinion	Statements of fact
______	______
______	______
______	______
______	______

3 Look back at the Model Essay on graffiti again.

- **a** In general, do you think the essay is more about what the writer thinks (opinion) or about what the writer knows (facts)? Is this appropriate to the essay question?____________________

  ____

- **b** Do you find the essay:

  very convincing? convincing? not convincing? not at all convincing?

  Why? If you did not find it convincing, what would have made it more convincing? ____________

  ____

- **c** Do you think the specific purpose of the essay is to:
  - argue a case or point of view? ____________________
  - discuss both sides of an issue or topic? ____________________
  - explain something? ____________________

3 How is an essay different from everyday speech and other written texts?

Where do you think each of these sentences comes from?

I swear it is true. You can ask her if you don't believe me.
Then suddenly the fields were bathed in a silvery light.
One hundred and fifty people were evacuated from their homes as the fires raged close to the town.
Youth are considerably more affected than adults by what they see in the media.

You probably said a conversation, a story, a newspaper report and an essay.

How did you know this? Well, you probably recognised something about the language in each. Every single time we communicate, we make choices about the words we use, and the way we put them together. We do this so that our communication will be successful. We think about:

- who we are talking or writing to – a close friend, a teacher, a stranger?
- the things we are talking about – the weather, personal feelings, a school subject?
- the method of communication – face-to-face, phone, a handwritten note, an essay?
- why we are communicating – to persuade, explain, entertain, instruct?

The difference between essays and speaking

When you write essays, you don't use the same words or organise your ideas in the way you would if you were talking to a friend at school. For example, you don't talk about personal feelings and experiences in an essay. Why not? One reason is because your purpose is to convince the reader, you need to sound sensible and objective and unswayed by personal experiences. Nor do you use slang or everyday colloquial language. Why not? One reason is that we only use such language when we are speaking or writing to people we are close to. Even though you might know your teachers very well, you are writing for them as teachers, not writing to them as friends.

The difference between essays and other written texts

You don't always write in exactly the same way. For example, in an essay you don't use imagery or descriptive language as you would in a story or a poem. Why not? Because you are not trying to evoke a picture in your reader's mind. Nor do you use numbers to list things as you would in a procedure. Why not? Because you are not trying to show your reader the order in which they should do something.

So, writing an essay is different from everyday conversation, and it is also different from other kinds of writing you do at school. In an essay, you need to choose your words and organise your ideas to be suited to:

- your general purpose to convince the reader and your specific purpose to argue, explain, discuss and so on
- a distant unknown audience
- the particular subject matter (eg. historical event, social issue, character in a novel)
- a formal written text.

Tasks

PAGES 99–100

1 Look back at the graffiti essay. If the writer were giving her view in a conversation to a friend she might use the sentences below (a-f).
Match the sentences with the paragraphs of the essay.
What are some of the differences you can see?

____

____

____

a I don't think tags and throw-ups are art but I reckon some graffiti is. ______

b Some guys I know are real artists but they don't get much of a chance to get better because there aren't enough legal walls. ______

c Look, I've thought about this a fair bit and I reckon that some graffiti – not all – is art. ______

d This suburb could look much better if they encouraged good graffiti. You don't seriously think that all graffiti is worse than old walls and dirty train carriages, do you? ______

e Let me tell you the difference between all the different sorts of graffiti you see around. ______

f Have you ever watched anyone do a real piece? I have, and it is pretty difficult. ______

2 Look at these extracts from four students' written texts. (*Note*: One is a speech script.)
Which do you think is an extract from an essay? Why? ______________________________

____

Where do you think the other extracts come from? ______________________________

____

What are some of the features you notice of the different types of writing?

____

____

____

a Over half of all adolescent girls try to lose weight. I researched many books, newspapers, pamphlets, videos, and magazines. However, I thought this article from the July 2000 edition of *Cosmopolitan* magazine was the most effective in depicting the dangers of dieting. In this article three women with anorexia nervosa recount their terrifying battle to fight this disease. Listen to what the first girl, Susanna, says ...

b And then the darkness came. Unlike the comforting fall of night this was a darkness cold and firm, closing its grip on her despite her every struggle. Then the screams. The blood curdling, terrifying screams of agony. The screams. The screams. The screams. Slowly fading into silence.

c The Doors were an American psychedelic rock group of the late 1960s. They were formed in 1965 with four band members: Jim Morrison, Ray Manzarek, Robby Krieger and John Densmore. Jim Morrison's extraordinary personality and talents were the major reason for the band's success. They combined classical rigour with freewheeling, jazzy improvisations.

d *The Colour of Magic* is the first book in the series *Discworld* by Terry Pratchett. It sets up a bizarre, imaginary world that is held up on the back of a turtle by four elephants. The story begins when a person called Twoflower comes on a ship to the city of Anhk Morpork in Discworld. He is the first tourist ever to do so.

e Some technological progress has not been beneficial for society. Instead it has returned us to our primeval, cavemen days. For example, weapons have caused many millions of people to die and have divided nations, families and individuals. The invention of implements of war has caused us to move away from the basic notions of civilisation developed over the centuries. Too many people have died for this to be seen as a benefit.

4 Are all essays the same?

OK, you know that essays are different from other writing. But does this mean that essays are all the same. The answer is **no**.

Unfortunately, some books on essay writing treat them as if they are the same. They treat **all** essays as argument essays and put great focus on the essay argument. I'd like to avoid this emphasis for two reasons.

Firstly, in everyday life 'argument' generally means a lot of emotional language and even shouting and fighting. This is definitely **not** the way things should go in an essay.

Secondly, there are many different kinds of essays that you have to write in high school. Sometimes you will be asked to 'argue' for one side of a case or the other (without shouting and getting emotional), but sometimes you will not.

Different kinds of essays

In the early years of secondary school you might need, instead, to explain something, to discuss ideas, to describe something, to compare and contrast two things, or to trace the history of something.

Sometimes you will be asked to do one of these things in order to do another. For example, you might be asked to compare and contrast two things in order to argue which is better. Or, you might be asked to trace the history of a period or event in order to give your opinion of its significance.

Understanding what you are asked to do is very important because it determines what sort of information and ideas you use and the way you organise them. (We have already mentioned this in Section 2 when talking about the specific purpose of your essay.)

Facts and opinions

You also know that most essays are a combination of facts and your own opinions on the topic. However, you will not have the same balance of fact and opinion in every essay.

In some essays you will have to use facts and figures more than your opinions. For example, essays in Geography or History are generally more about factual information. But even in these essays, your teachers expect you to bring your facts together, to interpret them and make a statement about them. If your teacher only wanted you to list facts, he or she would ask you to write something different – a report, for example.

In other essays you will have to use your own opinions and ideas more than facts. For example, essays in English are often more about your personal response to a text. But even in these essays, your teachers expect you to base your ideas on 'facts'. You will have to give evidence from the text (eg. a poem or a novel) that supports your personal response to it.

Tasks

PAGE 100

1 Look at these essay questions. The *topic* is the same as for the Model Essay on page 5 but the *type* of essay requested is not. In each case, say whether you think the essay question asks you to:

- argue a point of view (A)
- discuss both sides of an issue (D)
- explain something (E).

a How can we reduce graffiti vandalism? ______

b Is all graffiti vandalism? ______

c Like all art, spray can art requires technical skills. What are these? ______

d "There is no way to stop graffiti." Do you agree? ______

e What are the reasons for and against providing legal walls for graffiti artists? ______

2 Which of the following general statements would be suitable in response to each of the above?

i While most of the graffiti we see in our streets is undoubtedly vandalism, there are some outstanding exceptions. ______

ii Graffiti has been around for hundreds of years and will be around for hundreds more, no matter what is done to discourage it. ______

iii The best way to defeat graffiti vandalism is to provide legal spaces for young people to paint on but there are other ways too. ______

iv Spray can art is a method of painting requiring a range of high level technical skills. ______

v There are some very good reasons to provide legal graffiti walls, but there are also some good reasons not to. ______

3 Look at these paragraphs. Which one:

argues a point of view? ______ discusses both sides of an issue? ______ explains something? ______

a Video games develop physical reflexes and also strategic thinking and problem solving. At the same time, most games provide young people with hours of amusement. However, video games are not all good. In the first place, many games are violent and this can encourage children to be violent too. Secondly, children can become addicted to games if they are allowed to spend too much time on them.

b The growth of cities and the push for continuous economic growth has impacted on the environment in many ways. For example, deforestation is reducing tropical forests so that only fifty to sixty percent of natural forests remain in the world today. Newer threats such as global warming may be even more devastating.

c The nations of the developed world should stop investing money in space exploration. There are many urgent problems which could benefit from the huge amounts of money currently devoted to the space program. One problem is finding a way to feed the world's billions who cannot feed themselves. Another is education. There are millions of people in our world who still cannot go to school for one reason or another. There are also major environmental problems that would benefit from further research funding.

5 What is the basic essay structure?

The structure of most essays – no matter how long they are – is quite straightforward. The very simplest way to think about it is this:

The Introduction — you tell your reader what you are going to write about.
The Body — you write about it.
The Conclusion — you tell your reader what you have just written about.
Of course there is more to it than this, but this simple idea can help keep you on track as you write your essay. Let's imagine for a minute that your essay is like a large, dense forest.

The Introduction

If you were walking into this forest for the first time, you would be keen to find a signpost and probably a map to show you where you were going — in fact, you would be completely lost without these. The Introduction of your essay is the signpost to your ideas and a map of where you are going. Your reader – like you in the forest – would be lost without it.

So, in the Introduction, you tell the reader what the essay is about and what you are going to say. You relate back to the essay question and forward to what you are going to say about it. You offer a signpost (your main statement on the essay question) and usually a map to the points you will make.

The Body

Back to the forest. OK, you are now walking through it. There are lots of different types of trees and numerous tracks – some small, some large. It is hard to see where you are going. The Body of your essay is like this. It is full of your ideas and information.

Now, if you can't find the spaces or tracks between the trees, the map will be useless. Similarly, with your essay, if you put all your ideas in one big slab, your reader will find it hard to use the map in the Introduction. The reader won't be able to find their way through the 'forest' of ideas. So, you need to break up your ideas into manageable chunks or paragraphs.

Also, if you find that the forest is different from the map, you will be confused, probably get lost and give up. It is the same in your essay. If you write about something different from what you said you were going to write about (in your Introduction) your reader will be lost. So, your Body must match up with your Introduction.

The Conclusion

Now you are coming out of the forest. It has been a long journey and you have forgotten some of the things you saw. You find a board which thanks you for visiting the forest and shows you a photograph of the main attractions. This reminds you of your journey. In your essay, the Conclusion serves the same purpose. Essays are usually quite long pieces of writing and it helps to reminds your reader of what you have said and to pull it all together in a convincing way.

So, the Introduction-Body-Conclusion structure helps your reader keep track of your main idea and your supporting ideas. If your reader can keep track, he/she is more likely to be convinced by what you are saying – and that is your goal in writing.

Tasks

PAGE 100

1 Look back at the Model Essay on page 5 again.

Can you see:

- how the sentences in the Introduction prepare the reader for the Body Paragraphs?
- how the sentences in the Conclusion relate back to what was written in the Body Paragraphs?

Draw lines to show any connections you can see.

***

HELP!

PAGE 100

Look at this student's essay on the graffiti question. The student does not seem sure about what an essay is. Find at least five problems, and say what you would do to fix them.

Here are some questions to help you:

- Is there a clear statement which briefly and directly tells you the student's response to the essay question?
- Is the essay a combination of facts and opinions?
- Are all the ideas and information related to the essay question?
- Is the essay convincing?
- Does the essay address the essay question (ie. argue for or against)?
- Does the essay use the right kind of language for an essay?
- Is there an Introduction-Body-Conclusion structure?

Graffiti should be seen as a form of art. Do you agree or disagree?

Graffiti is everywhere I look. Like most people, I hate it. The other day I was walking to the shops and saw this boy take out a spray can and scribble all over the wall of some poor person's house. Terrible. When I told my mum she rang the police but of course it was too late. This person obviously did not care at all about the people who lived in the house and had to clear it up.

People who do graffiti should be made to clean up their work. As you can imagine, this is almost impossible because they usually do their work at night or when no one is around and so they usually don't get caught.

But if the police could catch them this would be the best solution. Other solutions would be to form neighbourhood groups to paint over their work. This happens in some places although it takes a lot of organisation.

While I have been writing this essay I have been thinking about some really good graffiti I have seen. I have to admit that some of it is actually artistic. Maybe the really good stuff should be allowed. But then how could you make different rules for different people? So in conclusion, I do not think graffiti is art and I do not think it should be allowed at all.

Prepare for writing

Teachers always tell you to prepare well for your writing. And they are right. Because essays are long pieces of writing, and contain many bits of information and many ideas, it is vital that you prepare well. The better you are prepared, the easier it will be to write the essay.

In this section, we will go step-by-step through five stages of preparation:

1 Understanding the essay question
2 Warming up the brain cells
3 Doing the research
4 Organising the content
5 Getting a plan together

To help us, we will go through the preparation process for three very different types of essay topics:

- *Explain how mobile phones affect our lives.*
- The Simpsons *does more than make us laugh. Do you agree or disagree?*
- *Books as we know them will disappear in the 21st century. Discuss.*

We will call these our Key Essay Questions.

(There are sample essays on these questions in the Extras section, page 95.)

We will also look back from time to time to our Model Essay on graffiti.

1 Understanding the essay question

As we've seen already, not every essay asks you to do the same task. So, it is absolutely essential that you read the essay question well, and think carefully about what you are being asked to do.

There are three important parts to most essay questions:

Topic words

There are words that tell you the topic. This might be, for example, a piece of literature, an historical event, a social trend, or an issue.

In the Model Essay on page 5, the topic was the issue of graffiti.

Focus words

Usually there are also focus words which narrow down the topic and tell you what particular aspect of the topic you are being asked to write about.

In the graffiti essay the focus words were: *should be seen as a form of art.*

Instruction words

Essay questions generally include a verb which gives you an instruction or tells you what you have to do — for example, *describe, explain, discuss, agree* or *disagree* with a statement, or *compare and contrast.*

But, not all essay questions include instruction verbs. Some are written as direct questions. For example:
What are the three most important ...?
How important was ...?
Do you think ...?

In these types of essay question, the instruction is contained in the question word.

In the graffiti essay there was no instruction verb telling you to argue for a point of view. Instead there was a direct question – *Do you agree or disagree?*

Direct question essays are especially common in Years 7-10, but it can be difficult to work out exactly what is required in response to them.

Because of this, you should **always** check with your teacher if you are not sure about what the essay question is asking you to do. Not every teacher uses the instruction verbs or questions in the same way.

HOT TIP!

It is a very good idea to look back regularly at the essay question as you plan and then write your essay. This will keep you on track in topic and task. If you go off the track, you might end up with a nice essay, but it will not be relevant to the set question. Essays that are not relevant are NOT given good marks.

Tasks

PAGE 100

1 Study the chart below which covers the main types of essays needed up to Year 10. Think about any essays you are doing at the moment. Which type are they?

instruction verbs	meaning	questions
describe	Give detail about the features or characteristics of something.	*What are/were/is/was?* *Who is/are/was/were?*
compare & contrast (usually both together)	Identify and discuss the similarities between two or more things (compare) and the differences between them (contrast).	*What are the advantages of X compared to Y?* *Is X more _____ than Y?* *What are the similarities and differences between X and Y?*
explain	Make plain, examine reasons, causes and/or effects.	*In what way does?* *What are the causes/effects of?* *How do/does?* *Why do/does?*
argue	Argue for one side of a given point of view (but show some awareness of the other side).	*Do you agree?* *Do you agree or disagree?* *Do you think?* *What was the most important?* *What do you think?*
trace or recount	Give a chronological account of events (say what happened first, second, third etc).	*What events led to?*
discuss	Give points for and against a point of view and come to a conclusion at the end of your essay based on these points.	*What are the points for and against?* *What are the pros and cons?* *How true is this?*

Notes:

1 Teachers sometimes use the instruction verb 'discuss' as a general term meaning 'write about'. So, take special care when you see this word in an essay question. Make sure you ask your teacher exactly what he or she expects you to do.

2 It can be difficult to decide if you should argue or discuss with some direct questions eg. How true is this? Again, always check what your teacher expects.

2 Look again at our three Key Essay Questions and the Model Essay question.

- The topic words are circled.
- The focus words – the words that narrow down the topic – are underlined.
- The instruction word or direct question which tells you what to do is marked with an asterisk(*).

Graffiti should be seen as a form of art. Do you agree or disagree?*

Explain how mobile phones affect our lives.*

The Simpsons does more than make us laugh. Do you agree or disagree?*

Books as we know them will disappear in the 21st century. Discuss.*

Now look at the essay questions below, and

- put a circle around the topic word/s
- underline the focus word/s
- asterisk the instruction word or direct question.

a Cloning will only bring disaster to mankind. Discuss.

b How does space exploration benefit the human race?

c What were some of the main differences between the ancient Olympic Games and the modern Olympic Games?

d Trace the development of popular music over any 20-year time period of the last century.

e Discrimination against youth is on the rise. Do you agree?

f What are the main causes of global warming?

g What events led to the French Revolution?

h Who was Alexander the Great and what were his major achievements?

3 Read the essay Introduction below and choose which of the essay questions (**a-d**) it is responding to.

______

Mankind has evolved over many millions of years. We originated from cavemen and apes, who wore leaves and ate each other. Whilst most progress since those days has been for the good, there has been some progress which has cost mankind dearly.

a How has mankind progressed over the past 10 000 years?

b Not all human progress is good progress. Do you agree?

c Trace the main stages of development of mankind over the past 10 000 years.

d Compare and contrast human life 10 000 years ago and human life today.

4 Now read this essay Introduction and choose the essay question it is responding to. ______

Most people would find it difficult to imagine life without television. They see it as a major source of information in their lives and rely on it for entertainment and relaxation. However, they may worry about its influence on their values and behaviour. Parents in particular might be concerned about its effect on their children. So, is television a good or bad influence in our lives? Should we consider throwing our TV sets away?

a Television is a great educator. Do you agree or disagree?

b Who invented television and what have been the major developments since its invention?

c We should all throw away our television sets. Discuss.

d Television is better than radio. Discuss.

5 Read this extract from a recent newspaper article and then do the task that follows.

> **CERTIFICATE STUDENTS ARE LOST FOR WORDS**
> **by Miranda Wood**
>
> Teachers marking the new School Certificate have found many students failed to understand basic terms used in the exams.
>
> Anthony Gorman, curriculum coordinator at Trinity Catholic College, Auburn, said markers were concerned at the number of students who didn't recognise key terms such as 'evaluate', 'compare' and 'contrast'.
>
> "Some students didn't quite know what the terms meant and failed to understand what the questions were asking," he said.
>
> (*The Sun-Herald*, 2/12/01, p. 26)

In the left-hand column below are some common essay instruction words. Although you might not be asked to do these essay tasks until senior secondary school, it is worth understanding them now.

Draw lines to match the instruction words with their meanings in the right-hand column. Use your dictionary to help you.

a. outline	i.	give concrete examples to show something clearly
b. analyse	ii.	break the topic up to show its nature, function, parts etc
c. justify	iii.	give the main points or features only
d. define	iv.	make critical observations
e. evaluate	v.	give the meaning of something
f. prove	vi.	give evidence or argument to show something is true
g. illustrate	vii.	show the connections between two or more things
h. relate	viii.	write about the worth of something in your view
i. review	ix.	explain why
j. comment	x.	same as evaluate
k. interpret	xi.	give good reasons for a decision or conclusion
l. examine	xii.	go over the main points and comment
m. account for	xiii.	bring out the meaning of something eg. an event
n. assess	xiv.	investigate in depth

2 Warming up the brain cells

Right. You have studied the essay question and think you understand it. What now? Well for most of us the next part is usually staring hopelessly at a blank piece of paper (or an empty computer document). Most of us need to get our brain cells warmed up on the topic.

Of course, most essays you do at high school will involve doing some research. But before you start doing the research to find out some facts and to find out what other people think, you should start with some ideas of your own.

These early ideas don't have to be brilliant or fantastic, and they don't have to be very detailed. No one will ever see them. They really are only to get your brain 'into gear'.

Getting some ideas down on paper before doing some research also gives you a starting point for your research – something concrete to look for.

Three ways to warm up those brain cells and get your ideas going are shown in this section:

- **brainstorming and mindmapping**
- **speedwriting**, and
- **asking WH- questions.**

There is no one right way to prepare. It's a good idea to try different ways and see what suits you best.

Here is what one student told me about how she gets started on an essay. Why don't you give it a try?

> *I have a good 'think' session. I lie down on my bed, or sit out in the sun, or have a long shower, and really think about the essay topic. If no one is around, I speak my thoughts out loud – to the ceiling, to the sun, to the bathroom walls. Sometimes I might try speaking them out loud to my mum or dad.*
> *I say things like:*
> *"Well, I definitely disagree with the statement. Why? Well, firstly I think blah blah blah. Secondly, I think blah blah blah ..." and so on.*
> *I don't worry about the details. I just try to give myself a framework – a sort of shell that I can fill in when I start writing. I usually change my ideas quite a bit as I write but at least I have something to start with.*

In this section we will practise warm-up strategies with the Key Essay Questions (on mobile phones, *The Simpsons* and the future of books).

HOT TIP!

Don't throw away your notes from this 'warm-up' stage. Put them somewhere safe so that you can go back to them from time to time as you plan and write. You might find them useful as you struggle to fill a paragraph much later on.

Tasks

1 Newspapers and magazines can be an excellent source of ideas for some essay topics. Look at the articles and headlines below on our three Key Essay Questions. They should help to warm up your brain cells on each topic.

Topic 1: Explain how mobile phones affect our lives.

Topic 2: *The Simpsons* does more than make us laugh. Do you agree or disagree?

Topic 3: Books as we know them will disappear in the 21st century. Discuss.

Topic 1

iv jst gt 2 get a msg 2U

It has been a month now since Brigina Mackay, 16, had her phone stolen on the train home from school, and things haven't got any easier. Since then, she has been unable to hold text-message conversations with her friends during class or SMS her boyfriend to say she misses him, and she has ... out on a month's worth of ... etter picture messages. ... e has to wait only until ... s Day before she gets a new ... d is back in the thick of ...

... put it this way, I was on ... I'd go through a $30 ... y, and that was mainly ... ages," she said. "Some ... ve conversations with; some it's like, meet me here at this time; other people it's like, a full conversation because you can't talk in class. All the time, during class, you sit there text messaging people, everyone does."

But it is the new-age love letters – love SMSs – that she sent to and received from her boyfriend that she misses the most. Unlike traditional love letters, SMS messages don't last forever. Once a phone's inbox reaches 30 messages, it's time to start culling. And it is romantic messages that often go, such as those Mackay received from her ex-boyfriend. "He quoted like Shakespeare and song lyrics and stuff like that, and they were really cute and ...

Katherine Dunn, 18, has been going out with her boyfriend James Behan, 25, for six weeks and they message each other whenever they can. "It used to be every day, until I got a bar on my phone for making too many calls," said Dunn.

"You have to go through the favourite [messages] and keep the favourites and go through from there, like the least favourite, get rid of them."

Behan likes to keep all the messages from Dunn, and thinks a memory disk he could transfer them to would be really useful.

"That'd be great, wouldn't it, because then you could ...

6 News | Wednesday, February 13, 2002 | smh.com.

Deal at last over stolen mobiles ban

Sue Lowe

Lost and stolen mobile phones may finally be banned from all mobile networks, following a meeting yesterday between the mobile carriers and law enforcement agencies.

Under the plan agreed to yesterday, carriers will use the International Mobile Equipment Identity (IMEI) code built into every mobile phone to identify and blacklist stolen phones. All carriers have agreed to ban blacklisted phones from their network.

It has taken consumer groups, the police and government over three years to get this far – in which time an estimated 240,000 mobile phones have been stolen – but it could be months before any solutions are implemented.

According to the Australian Mobile Telecommunications Association (AMTA), which represents the mobile industry, about 2000 mobile phones are now reported lost or stolen every week.

Over 85 per cent of those are estimated to end up reconnected to other networks, generating millions of dollars in revenue for the carriers.

Legislative changes were also reco... ...ded, including a move ... ...ing with IMEI ... Soft- ... with the number of an obsolete handset. This is not illegal.

Both technical and legislative working groups will report back to a steering committee by the end of May, but beyond that no-one is prepared to estimate how long it will be before changes are put in place.

One of the arguments carriers have used against blocking IMEI numbers is that they are not unique, meaning scores of phone users could find their handset blocked.

Telstra spokesman, Tim Scott, said the duplication risk would require sophisticated customer management, so that innocent customers could be contacted in advance and have their handset swapped.

But at least one expert has dismissed this as a delaying tactic.

Reg Robertson, who was contracted by AMTA 18 months ago to develop and run the Find-a-phone database, claims there is not one duplica... IMEI codes or ... which is design... mobiles with th...

Mr Robertso... doubt that the ... survive as lack ... from Telstra an... ning stolen phon... it inoperable.

He had stopped taking a $22 fee from subscribers because he couldn't provide the promised service, and is now suing the AMTA over failure to meet the ... the contract.

Love in the time of mobiles

So you are holding out against the mobile scourge? Give in. They are ... ay. And, as ***Lauren Martin*** *... rites, the changes they have wrought affect everyone.*

I ... the ex by ... message has become the chic way to end a relationship. In the United Arab Emirates, it's the sheik way to get a divorce. Truly. While Islamic law says men must declare the end by saying "I divorce you" three times, a court in Dubai set a precedent for allowing the sentiment to be delivered via text message over a mobile phone.

The no-fuss bust-up plan got the blessing of a senior Malaysian cleric, too, though a prominent female politician there is campaigning against it.

Mobile phones are changing everything, everywhere. Seduction, school, ...

families who don't have a lot of money. It's like having a car – only the most disadvantaged people in our community don't have cars; they're regarded as essential. Mobile phones are going that way."

Even the penitent Franciscan friars have a phone habit now. The monks, who dedicate themselves to missionary and humanitarian work, engaged a Milan designer to create new robes for them. According to *The Times*, they've updated to a snappy charcoal grey number in lightweight wool, with breast pockets for their mobile phones.

THE mobile market is not for corporate big shots any more. While profession... the busine...

Parents paying off kids' phone debts

Mobile phones to be even smarter

Mobile phones of the future look like being even more expensive than they are now, but at least they will be smarter to make up for the increase in price.

Mobile phone may lead to killer

Police investigating the recent double murder on the NSW South Coast coast believe that a mobile phone call made to a number could be the lead they are looking for.

No hiding place

Mobile phone users can now be pinpointed with accuracy of a few metres.

Topic 2

Simpsons offer 'moral orientation'

The Simpsons could help provide 'moral orientation' for those pondering the meaning of life, according to a Scottish academic.

Dr Kris Jozajtis, from Stirling University, said the cult television cartoon offered an ideal reference point to help religious teachers discuss morality.

Wahoo! Simpsons celebrate 10 years

The Simpsons, the cult cartoon that changed the face of TV, is celebrating its 10th birthday with a bash that included getting a sta... the Hollywood Walk of F...

Simpsons 'more interesting' than Royalty

Young people find the cartoon Simps... family more interesting than the Royal ... according to a survey of 16 t... ...t of those surveyed l... said they were interes... ...o said the same abou...

Simpsons revealed as models of family values

A scholar's praise: 'An enduring image of the nuclear family' embedded in satire.

D'oh! Homer and Bart Simpson as upholders of family values?

Don't have a cow, man. An English professor says it's true. In a recent issue of ...

Top dad Homer 'icon for Blair'

Tony Blair leads a country — Homer Simpson leads a life devoted to doughnuts.

Tony Blair hob-nobs with heads of state — Homer hangs out in a dive bar.

So when Mr Blair is a father again next year, who should he look to as a role model?

Yes, Homer Simpson!

Topic 3

YOU GOT THE BOOK

You may not be able to cuddle up with them, but the next generation of ...

the product pitch is at people who r... for pleasure, but as part of their ... professionals, academics and stud... That's quite a...

A platform ideal for trai...

EXPERIENCED commuters making the daily train trek to the city know to pack a paperback in case of delays. ... ass the time as well as a good ... books at hand – ...

documents). Because D... smaller than plain text ... readily on your hand-he... range of reader-friendly ... bookmarks for saving y... The Doc e-texts are t... PRC files that are instal... ... other Palm...

Britannica unbound as books abandoned

After more than 200 years, the Encyclopaedia Britannica has stopped printing books because its CD-ROM version is a far bigger seller.

It sells only a minimal number of books, compared with 150,000 CD-ROMs every year in Europe alone.

A full set of the bound volumes costs about $1,400 while the computerised version, containing the same information, is $199.

The company was founded in 1768 in Edinburgh and first drafts of the encyclopedia were printed three years later. It is now based in Chicago.

The British manag...

...version than ever bought the books, and consumers also find it more user-friendly. ... bought the computerised ...

Press Association

Sign of the tomes

Hand-held e-books can now match the look and feel (if not the smell) of paper-based works. **Keith Austin** turns the page on a very modern story.

THERE'S a romance about what could be called the Codex Age that goes beyond logic and into obsession. Since the Church dumped the awkward scroll in favour of the user-friendly codex – a bundle of pages stitched together – about 1,600 years ago, ...

Books: facing their final chapter?

... At the moment, an author will take 10 ... selling at $29.95 ...

he or she is losing out. That's something we are going to have to look at very carefully." Someone else who has experienced the ... eBook first-hand is Richard Tardif, ... Not, the Macquarie ...

... $US4; Peanut Press ... has sci-fi titles and myst... about $US7. ... vices employs ... name, this ... Word

Books are bound to change

The e-book. Cheaper, yes. Better? Maybe, writes **Sarah Bryden-Brown**

NOT all new technology means certain death for its predecessor. Sometimes, in fact, technology can breathe another robust chapter into the life of an age-old existence. And so it is with e-books and e-publishing.

E-books are electronic books downloaded from the internet to be read on either a computer or handheld reader. Putting aside the cost of the hardware, they are cheaper than p-books and with the recent launch of the ebookman, a hand-held device used to read material, their place in publishing is expected to take off.

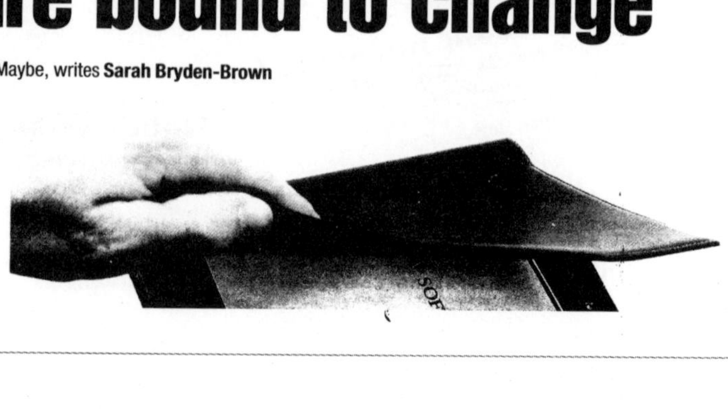

Brainstorming is a good way to start on an essay. It means writing down everything you think or know about the topic in point or note form. You might not end up using all that your write down but that doesn't matter. The important thing is to get the ideas down and not worry too much about whether they are right or wrong, useful or not useful. You should write as much as you can. When you have finished, you can link up your ideas with arrows and circles.

Mindmapping is a more structured form of brainstorming. Instead of writing down just anything you can think of, you think of some key ideas and then jot down related ideas. Some people find it easier to go straight into this more organised way of brainstorming.

2 **a** Look at this student's brainstormed notes on the mobile phones Key Essay Question:

Mobile phones

less privacy

noisy

convenient in emergencies

waste time

better communication

compare olden days

irritating on public transport

b Add your own ideas to the list. Use the headlines and articles on the previous page to help you.

Remember: Don't worry about how useful your ideas will be. The aim is to get the brain cells working!

c Link up any ideas that seem related or overlapping.

3 Look at this student's mindmap to start off on the future of books Key Essay Question. Add your own ideas.

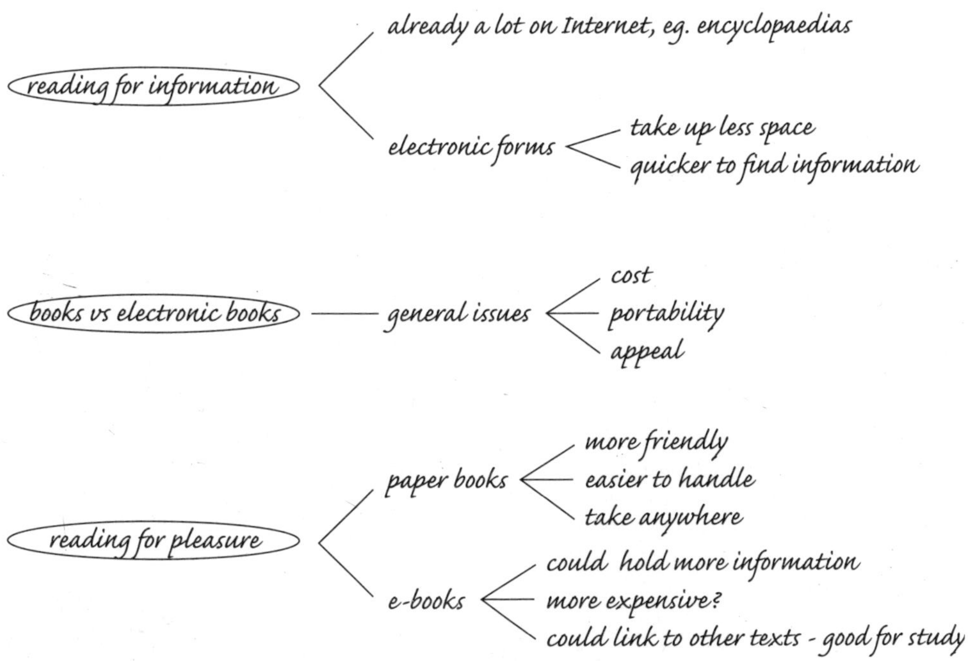

3 Now, on own paper, brainstorm or mindmap for *The Simpsons* essay question.

Speedwriting

Speedwriting is where you give yourself a time limit, say five minutes, to write as much as you can on the essay question. Don't worry about grammar and punctuation. Keep writing until the time is up. Like brainstorming, this exercise warms up the brain cells, but it also forces you to think about the topic and task. Some of your ideas may end up in your essay but others will probably not make it that far.

4 Look at this student's speedwriting on Topic 2.

I watch The Simpsons every week at least once — everyone I know loves them. Why so popular? Could this be related to question—because more than a comedy? Mum used to complain about me watching it but she did not really know what it was about. Then one day she sat down and watched it and now she thinks it's one of the best shows around. She loves Homer though she complains when Dad does similar things. I think the characters are so hopeless that we love them. What does this mean?

5 Speedwrite on the other two essay topics for about five minutes.

Explain how mobile phones affect our lives.

____

____

____

____

____

____

Books as we know them will disappear in the 21st century. Discuss.

____

____

____

____

____

____

Asking Wh- questions

Wh- questions are questions beginning with *What, Who, When, Where, How* or *Why*. Writing questions like this can help you get going with most essay topics. Sometimes they can end up being the basis of a good essay plan.

6 Here are some Wh- questions on the mobile phone topic. Can you add any more?

What are mobile phones?
Who uses them most?
When do they use them?
When are they useful?
How many people use them?

____

____

How long have we been using them?
Where do they use them?
Why do they use them?
When are they a nuisance?
What are their disadvantages?

____

____

7 Now write some Wh- questions on the other two Key Essay Questions on your own paper.

3 Doing the research

OK. You have had a 'think' session and used some strategies to get your own ideas going. Now is the time to go and look for some facts and for other people's ideas on the topic – in other words, do the research.

Of course a lot of your information will come from your teachers in class lessons and – depending on the topic – from conversations with friends and family.

Here I want to focus on getting ideas from written texts – books, websites and newspapers. In other words, through reading.

It is not possible to cover all the reading skills you need when researching. I want to focus on two areas of difficulty that students have: selecting information and then working out how reliable it is.

Selecting information

Often the problem is not that you can't find the information – it is that you find too much.

> *I like doing the research – it's easy to find stuff and I feel like I'm getting somewhere – but pretty soon I start to feel overwhelmed. I'm supposed to be writing about 300 words and I've printed off heaps of pages from about 10 websites and found about 6 library books that have something on the topic. Suddenly I feel like I can't do it. I feel swamped.*

Like many students, this student needs to find a way to select. Two skills that she needs are **skimming** and **scanning**.

Working out how reliable the information is

A second common problem is working out how much you can depend on the information — whether it is right, how up-to-date it is, whether it is biased in some way. This is especially important these days with so much research being done through Internet websites.

To work out how reliable information is you need to read critically.

HOT TIP!

When you are looking for useful material for your essay, always have the essay question RIGHT IN FRONT OF YOUR EYES. Write it on a post-it pad and stick it on the side of the computer if you are using the Internet. Or, stick it on your folder if you are looking for books in the library.

Keep looking back to the question and asking yourself:

- **Is this material really on the topic?**
- **Is it on the particular focus area of the topic?**
- **Is this material related to the task? For example, does it give me information that will help me argue, explain, compare and contrast etc?**

STEP 2

Tasks

PAGES 100–101

Skimming

Skimming means looking quickly over a text to get a general idea of what it's about. You:

- **don't** look at every word
- **do** look at pictures, headings and highlighted words
- **do** read the first paragraph of the text (and maybe the first sentences of some other paragraphs)
- **don't** worry about words or parts of text you don't understand.

If you can skim-read, you save yourself a lot of work. You don't take home 40 books from the library when only three would do. You don't spend time reading through texts that end up being no use to you in your essay writing.

1 Often the first paragraph of a text gives us a lot of information about what is in the text.

Read this first paragraph from a website text on the future of books. Decide if the main idea of the text is likely to be:

- the possibilities for electronic books ______
- the disadvantages of electronic books ______
- the disadvantages of paper books. ______

***The Future of Books* by Doug Johnson**

I enjoyed the recent LM_NET discussion of the impact of technology on the future of books. But I think too many of the responses gave us an 'either or' scenario: we will either have books OR technology. Maybe we should consider printing itself a technology – a technology that is also evolving.

2 Now skim the rest of *The Future of Books* text for 30 seconds. **Do not read every word!**

What do you now think is the main idea?______________________________

____

Were you right or wrong in your prediction above?______________________

The technology of the "book" has already seen a number of transitions: from clay to wax to papyrus to vellum to cloth to paper, stored as tablets or scrolls or folios or books, bound in horn or leather or cloth or paper. Standardized spelling, paragraphs, and punctuation are all relatively new inventions in written communication – as are hyperlinks!

While, like most of you, I would certainly mourn the passing of the function "books", I would rejoice if well-designed silicon replaced cellulose as the means for publishing them.

Let's face it. Our current paper printed books (with rare and expensive exceptions among those for children's and art's sake) are a pretty shoddy mess: rapidly disintegrating spines, greasy feeling paper, squinty print, shoddy color separation, subject to acid disintegration, easily damaged, quickly out of print, bulky to store, back-breaking to move, mouldy smelling and visually dull. While I am as sentimental as the next person about the memories particular books evoke, I like to believe it is really the excitement of the story, the perspective of the author, or the lyricism of the language to which I am reacting. I don't remember the color of a favorite book's spine.

If paper is passe, what might be the advantages of the digitized book in a form more mature than the primitive Sony Bookman or the cumbersome CD-ROM encyclopedia on the desktop computer? I think I can envision a new kind of book with which I can cuddle up in bed. Stealing from the reports of the developing technologies, here's one possible version of an e-book.

Imagine opening a padded notebook bound in calfskin. It weighs little, smells good, and is available in a variety of sizes. It runs on a watch battery which needs replacing once every three years, and has a solar panel like those in calculators. On one side is a softly glowing, back-lit, glare-free screen. My wife can sleep while I read in bed. I think my page's background would be a rich ivory color. On the other side is a small keyboard, a number of buttons and a network jack.

The e-book's screen offers several improvements over the static printed page. The text's font can be changed to suit one's tastes and the size adjusted for aging eyes. My wife insists her screen will have built-in correction so she need not wear her glasses when reading. The page displays full-color illustrations, of course.

Come across an unfamiliar word? Touch it and the glossary key to the right of the screen and a brief definition pops up. Many books will come with a picture and sound glossary. Touch the word, see the object, character or setting.

Eyes really tired? Switch to the text reader. No robotic-sounding Talking Moose voice in my e-book. My book has my favourite actors and actresses as narrators. I can buy voices the way I currently buy fonts. I also get to choose how much interpretation the reader gives the story. I like a straight reading, but others may want a full-blown dramatization.

Doodle in the margins? You bet, with a pen on the touch-sensitive screen or via the keyboard on electronic sticky notes. I can search my notes as well as the text for the particularly pertinent passage. Set referenced bookmarks? Certainly.

My book isn't just one book. It's at least a backpack full (plus all standard reference sources), all of which have been downloaded from the local bookshop for a fraction of the cost of the paper version because I'm not buying paper, which is expensive to make, bind into books, store, transport and shelve. My e-book means never having to say "out of print" . The books are stored into the computer on a chip that holds amounts of information currently unattainable even on the biggest hard drive.

The less tradition-bound readers may even expect and use some content flexibility. Main character's name the same as your least favourite person, which spoils the mood? Do a little find-and-replace, and "Call me Ishmael" becomes "Call me Ralph" (or whatever). Set the latest Stephen King to mild, scary, or terrifying. Like happy endings? Select that version.

We've all seen the potential that digitized information has had for education: computer-assisted instruction, multi-media books for beginner readers and of course the Internet.

Nothing novel here, but for those who are and always will be readers, a digital future has exciting possibilities. Send me your ideas about what features your e-book should have. I'll add them next time.

Doug Johnson is the district Media Supervisor for the Mankato Public Schools, Mankato, Minnesota.

Last updated: February 6, 1998.
http://www.4j.lane.edu/cybrary/futurebooks.html

3 Now skim the text for another 30 seconds and then cover it.

Does the text have ideas relevant to the essay question? ____________________

Jot down below any ideas you remember that might be useful.

____

____

____

STEP 2

Scanning

Scanning is when we look through a text to find a particular piece of information. We usually have an idea of what we are looking for. We:

- **do not** look at every word
- **do not** bother about understanding the overall meaning
- **do** run our eyes over the page very quickly
- **do** look only for the words or numbers we are interested in
- **do** ignore the rest of the text.

Scanning is particularly important when we need to find a fact or idea to support an idea we want to include in an essay.

4 Look back at the *The Future of Books* text. Scan to find the answers to these questions. Do this as quickly as you can.

a What does the author say are new inventions in written communication?

b List three disadvantages of paper books mentioned.

c What is the writer's vision of an e-book based on?

d What sort of battery would his e-book run on? __________

e Why would his e-book be good for his eyes?

f What feature could you use if you started falling asleep?

g Could you write notes on his e-book? __________

5 Look again at the text. Find at least one idea or fact to support these statements.

a You could take electronic books to bed. __________

b Electronic books would be more economical than paper books. __________

c The potential for electronic forms of information can be seen already. __________

Reading critically

- It is important to realise that not everything you read is true or reasonable. Facts may be left out or twisted to suit the writer's views, or even be incorrect. Opinions may be biased or illogical.
- You need to be critical in **all** the reading you do, but it is perhaps most important when reading websites. Thousands of people put information and ideas on the Internet. They don't need to have any qualifications or special knowledge to do so. Sometimes there is no information about who the author of a website is.
- At least with a book, you usually know who the author is and in most cases, can presume they know something about the topic, given that they have managed to get someone to publish their work.
- Newspaper and magazine articles are different again. We usually know who the author is, but we have to think about the reliability of the information. As people say "You can't always believe what you read in the newspaper". News reports sometimes contain inaccurate information or carefully selected facts and ideas to make a point. Also, some newspapers and magazines have better reputations for truth and accuracy than others.
- So, what can we do? When reading any text:
  - Take notice of who the author is, or which organisation he/she represents, if this information is given.
  - Think about how this might influence what the author has written.
  - Take notice of when the text was written or the website developed or last updated, especially if using facts and figures from it.
  - Look at a range of texts on the topic in order to compare the facts or ideas you find.

STEP 2

6 Look again at the text *The Future of Books*.

Who is the author? Is he:

- an expert of some sort (eg. technology, electronic publishing, education)? ______________
- an interested member of the community? ______________
- a person representing a company which makes books? ______________
- a journalist? ______________

How does your knowledge of the author affect the way you would use this information? That is, would you quote him as an expert? Would you use the text to give you ideas? Would you use what he says to prove a point? ______________

____

____

When was the text written? How would this affect the way you used it? ______________

____

____

7 In the Extras section at the back of the book, there is some stimulus material on each of the three Key Essay Questions.

a Skim the material now for its general usefulness for the essay topics.

b Scan the material to find any especially useful facts and ideas and underline them.

c Read the material, thinking carefully about who wrote it, where it is from, and what this means for your use of it in your essay.

8 Do your own research on one or more of the three Key Essay Questions over the next few days. Use books and websites, but also look out for useful newspaper articles.

4 Organising your ideas

One of the biggest problems that students have in essay writing is working out how to divide up all they want to say into smaller and more manageable chunks.

Usually they have this difficulty because they start writing without thinking about how they are going to do it.

Let me say this to you loud and clear. The time to think about how to organise the essay content is when you are **preparing** to write. It is, without a doubt, one of **the most important things** you must think about. It is important in any long piece of writing. In essays, it is crucial.

Why important?

If you divide up and organise your ideas in a clear and logical way for the essay question it will:

- stop **you** rambling on and going off the essay question, and
- help **your reader** follow your ideas and be convinced by them.

Organisation and essay purpose

In every essay, you will start with an Introduction and end with a Conclusion, but the specific purpose of your essay will determine how you divide up and organise the Body of your essay.

In other words, it will depend on the instruction word or direct question word in the essay question. Is your purpose, for example, to argue a case, to explain something, to discuss arguments for and against, or to compare and contrast?

For example, if you are explaining why something happens, you won't achieve your purpose by organising the Body into arguments for and against an idea. You will achieve it by organising it into different causes or reasons. If you are tracing the history of something, you won't achieve your purpose by organising the Body according to the reasons certain events happened. You will achieve it by dividing it up into events or periods.

Important organisational patterns

In this section we will look at the important patterns of organisation that you will need in essay writing. We will focus especially on the organisation of argument essays, discussion essays and explanation essays because they are the main types of essays (as reflected in our Key Essay Questions).

Believe me, if you organise your ideas well, your essays will stand out from the rest.

HOT TIP!

Sometimes the essay question helps you to divide up the topic by asking you three or four specific questions. When this is so, you should always use the separate questions as your main essay divisions.

Tasks

A PAGE 101

1 Study the chart below. It shows how common essay types are typically organised. Long and complicated essays may include more than one pattern. For example, there may be a comparison/contrast of two things as part of an argument. But generally, these basic patterns will be the core structure of even the most complicated essays. **Remember**: we are talking about organising the **Body** only. These patterns will always follow an Introduction and be followed by a Conclusion.

essay type	typical organisational pattern	example
describe	• feature or aspect 1 • feature or aspect 2 • feature or aspect 3 etc	***What are the features of Thai cooking?*** • *main cooking methods* • *main cooking utensils* • *use of herbs and spices* • *ingredients*
compare & contrast	• area of comparison/contrast 1 - one thing being compared - the other thing being compared • area of comparison/contrast 2 - one thing - the other thing • area of comparison/contrast 3 - one thing - the other thing etc	***Compare and contrast living now and in your parents' day.*** • *entertainment* — *parents' day* — *now* • *transport* — *parents' day* — *now* • *housework* — *parents' day* — *now* • *clothing* — *parents' day* — *now*
explain	• cause, effect, reason, or factor 1 • cause, effect, reason, or factor 2 • cause, effect, reason, or factor 3 etc	***What are the main causes of global warming?*** • *increasing world population* • *increased use of fossil fuels* • *increasing use of motor vehicles* • *more agriculture and land clearing*
argue	• argument for an opposing view and a comment on this view (optional) • argument 1 for your view • argument 2 • argument 3 etc	***Is discrimination against youth on the rise?*** • *youth create negative attitudes – true in some cases* • *new laws specially target youth* • *few recreation facilities for youth* • *youth treated differently by authorities eg. on trains*
trace or recount	• event or period 1 • event or period 2 • event or period 2 etc	***What events led to the French Revolution?*** • *ordinary people's demands not met* • *creation of the National Assembly* • *increasing anger and discontent* • *meeting hall locked and swearing of oath to resist*

discuss	• argument 1 for the idea • argument 2 for etc • argument 1 against the idea • argument 2 against etc	***Cloning will bring disaster to mankind. Discuss.*** • *against laws of nature* • *potential for unethical, even evil use* • *difficult to control* • *just another scientific advance* • *potential for fighting disease* • *strict ethical guidelines should be possible*
	OR argument for argument against argument for argument against etc	OR • *against laws of nature* • *just another scientific advance* • *potential for unethical, even evil use* • *potential for fighting disease* • *difficult to control* • *strict ethical guidelines should be possible*

Argument essays

- Argument essays generally ask you to present a case for one side of an issue.
- You need to **clearly state which side you are on** in the Introduction.
- However, you don't always have to totally agree or disagree with the statement in the question. You can have a view somewhere in between, but you must argue for this view and not just 'sit on the fence'.
- You may need to clarify what the issue is, or define key words in the question before you start on the main paragraphs of the Body – especially if you are not totally agreeing or disagreeing.
- It can be a good idea to include one argument on the opposing side to show you are aware of this view, and to add a comment which rebuts it. You can do this straight after the Introduction or just before the Conclusion.
- You will generally use both fact and opinion. In literature essays the 'fact' will often be evidence from a story or poem which supports your opinion.
- Argument essays are more commonly asked for in English, Drama and History than in other subjects.

2 Look back at the graffiti essay on page 5 (an argument essay).

Does the writer totally agree with the statement in the essay question, totally disagree, or have a view somewhere in between? ____________________

Is there a paragraph to clarify or define the topic? If so, which paragraph? ____________________

Why does the writer see a need to clarify or define anything? ____________________

____

____

Is there an argument for a view that opposes the writer's? If so, in which paragraph? ____________________

How many arguments does the writer give to support her view on the topic? ____________________

What are the arguments?

____

____

____

3 Look at the argument essay pattern in the chart above. Practise organising argument essays by quickly jotting down three arguments to argue for **or** against one of these statements. If you can, include one argument for the opposing view that you think you should comment on. (Choose more than one topic if you want extra practice.)

Cats make better pets than dogs.
Homework should be banned.
All zoos should be closed immediately.

(argument for opposing view and comment ____________________)

argument 1 for your view ____________________

argument 2 ____________________

argument 3 ____________________

4 Think now about the Key Essay Question which asks you to argue a case: The Simpsons *does more than make us laugh. Do you agree or disagree*?

Here is how one student approached the organisation of ideas for this essay. He agreed with the statement in the essay question and gave three reasons and one example of an episode to support each reason.

argument 1 - shows us the importance of family – one example
argument 2 - makes us think about what life is all about – one example
argument 3 - teaches us how we should behave towards each other – one example

There are many other ways to approach the task and many other arguments you could use. Use your own ideas to jot down another possible way and another set of arguments.

argument for opposing view and comment ____________________

argument 1 for your view ____________________

argument 2 ____________________

argument 3 ____________________

Explanation essays

- Explanation essays generally ask you to explain a process, phenomenon, trend or situation.
- They ask you to talk about causes, effects, reasons or factors. More complicated explanation essays might ask you to talk about both causes and effects.
- You do **not** have to argue for a point of view in an explanation essay.
- You often need to define the phenomenon, trend, or process being explained either in the Introduction on in the paragraph just after it.
- You will generally use more fact than opinion.
- Explanation essays are more commonly asked for in History, Geography and the Social Sciences than in English, although English questions on writer's techniques are explanations.

5 Look back at the chart to check how you would organise an explanation essay. Practise organising ideas for explanation essays by quickly jotting down answers to one of these questions. (Choose more than one topic if you want extra practice.)

How does sport benefit us?
Why do people take up smoking?
What are the main causes of air pollution?

cause, effect, reason, or factor 1 ____________________

cause, effect, reason, or factor 2 ____________________

cause, effect, reason, or factor 3 ____________________

6 Think now about the Key Essay Question which asks you to explain something: *Explain how mobile phones affect our lives.*

Here is how one student approached the organisation of ideas for this essay. He gave two positive effects and then two negative effects of mobile phones.

effect 1 (positive) – make everyday events more convenient
effect 2 (positive) – make it easier for people to phone emergency services
effect 3 (negative) – make it difficult to have privacy
effect 4 (negative) – intrude on other people's lives when you use them

There are many other ways to approach the task and many other effects you could mention. Use your own ideas to jot down another possible way.

effect 1 ______________________________

effect 2 ______________________________

effect 3 ______________________________

Discussion essays

- Discussion essays generally ask you to give arguments on both sides of the issue and then to give your overall opinion at the end of your essay in the Conclusion.
- Although you have usually formed your opinion before you start writing, you don't show this. By doing this, you are saying to your reader: *I have now weighed up all these arguments for and against, and here is what I have concluded.*
- You need to **clearly state your overall opinion** on the essay question in your Conclusion. As with argument essays it may not be clearly one side or the other – it may be somewhere in between.
- Some discussion essay questions are not so much the 'arguments for and against' kind. Instead they are 'the issues around' kind. For example, *Discuss the significance of body image in modern society*.
- The word *discuss* is used in all sorts of ways, so it is always wise to check what your teacher wants from an essay.
- Discussion essays are more commonly asked for in English, History and Economics than in other subjects.

7 Look back at the chart to check how you would organise a discussion essay. Practise organising ideas for discussion essays by quickly jotting down points for and against one of the statements below. Then decide which side you agree with after considering the arguments on both sides. (Choose more than one topic if you want extra practice.)

Progress always benefits mankind.
TV violence leads to viewer violence.
We should all speak English.

argument 1 for the idea ______________________________

argument 2 for the idea ______________________________

argument 1 against the idea ______________________________

argument 2 against ______________________________

final opinion ______________________________

8 Look at the Key Essay Question which asks you to discuss something: *Books as we know them will disappear in the 21st century. Discuss.*

Here is how one student approached the organisation of ideas for this essay.

argument for — Increasing use of the Internet for researching information
argument against — Internet has disadvantages eg. difficulty and unreliability of information
argument against — Books commonly used for enjoyment
argument for — Paper books not good for environment
overall opinion — We will use books less but they will not disappear

Note: This student has departed from the typical pattern (as in chart), putting arguments for, against, against, for, instead of arguments for, against, for, against etc. This is OK if it works better for what she wants to say.

Use your own ideas to jot down another possible set of arguments (using either pattern).

argument 1 for the idea ______________________________

argument 2 for the idea ______________________________

etc ______________________________

argument 1 against ______________________________

argument 2 against ______________________________

etc ______________________________

OR

argument for ______________________________

argument against ______________________________

argument for ______________________________

argument against ______________________________

etc ______________________________

5 Doing a detailed plan

So you have done your research and you have got some ideas for your essay. You have thought about how to organise your ideas to suit the essay purpose.

What now? Well now it is time to properly plan your whole essay.

Everyone is different

Students are always told to plan their essays before they start. This is good advice. But, everybody is different and not everyone can start with a nice formal plan. Some students have to start writing the actual essay to get any sort of plan going in their head. But even these people usually need to stop writing once they get going and jot down notes about where they are going from that point on.

Some students like quite detailed plans. Others are happy to start writing once they have a very broad organisational plan in place, like those in the previous section. Some like them neat and tidy before they start writing. Others are happy with very messy plans. Some like numbers and letters. Others like visual plans.

Why plan?

Even if you think that plans are just not for you, it is a good idea to get practice with them. You will definitely need them in senior secondary years when essays are more complicated and often need to be written in exam conditions.

Whichever way you go about your plan, the important thing is that you do one, because it helps you 'see' the essay as one whole piece **before** and **as** you write.

Your plan is like a road map you might use in a strange area. It shows you:

- where you are starting from (the essay question and the Introduction)
- where you are going to (the Conclusion), and
- how you are going to get there (the Body).

Your plan helps you to stick to the main idea which is holding your essay together and reminds you that all the smaller ideas need to connect to this main idea.

Sometimes you might end up going away from your plan when you start writing, because the actual process of writing develops your thinking on the topic and task. This is perfectly fine as long as there is a good reason. It is a bit like starting off on a journey following a good map, but finding at some point in the journey that there is a better route to take.

HOT TIP!

Put your plan where you can always find it and see it. Good ideas sometimes come at the oddest times, and it is good to be able to get hold of your plan and add the ideas when they are fresh in your mind. Maybe have a couple of copies of your plan – one at home and one at school for extra convenience.

1 In Task 2 in the last section you looked at the organisation of ideas in the model essay on graffiti. A broad organisational plan for that essay (body only) might look like this:

paragraph 1 — define and clarify different kinds of graffiti

paragraph 2 — argument 1 – good graffiti improves the look of our streets

paragraph 3 — argument 2 – real graffiti pieces take great artistic skill

paragraph 4 — argument 3 – recognition of graffiti as art would give young artists the chance to develop skills and contribute to community

Look at how this broad plan has been expanded below for paragraphs 1 and 2. Add detail for paragraphs 3 and 4 using the graffiti essay as your guide.

Introduction

- frequent complaints in media
- basic graffiti forms are not art but complex forms are
- complex forms take skill
- brighten up streets
- give young artists opportunities to develop skills and so good for community

paragraph 1 — distinguish between three types of graffiti:
- tags, throw-ups and pieces
- most graffiti first two types – not art
- last type is art

paragraph 2 — argument 1 – good graffiti potential to improve streets and transport:
- colourful, attractive
- looks better than old surfaces – walls, trains
- often painted over because seen as vandalism

paragraph 3 — argument 2 – real pieces take artistic skill to design and carry out

____

____

____

____

paragraph 4 — argument 3 – recognition as art would give artists the chance to develop skills

____

____

____

____

2 In the last section you looked at broad organisational plans for each of the Key Essay Questions. On the next page you can see how each of those plans could be expanded into detailed essay plans.

Study these plans now.

The Simpsons does more than make us laugh. Do you agree or disagree?

Broad organisational plan

argument 1 — shows us the importance of family – one example

argument 2 — makes us think about what life is all about – one example

argument 3 — teaches us how we should behave towards each other – one example

More detailed plan

Intro — *Simpsons* does more than make us laugh because it teaches us moral lessons – episode examples

para 1 — shows us the importance of family – family dog episode

- family dog needs expensive operation
- family make sacrifices to pay for it
- teaches us family more important than material objects

para 2 — makes us think about what life is all about – blowfish episode

- Homer swallows blowfish
- doctor gives him 24 hours to live
- Homer does everything he ever wanted
- doctor's wrong and Homer OK
- teaches us to value our lives

para 3 — teaches us how we should behave towards each other – Mr Burns episode

- Mr Burns shot and tells everyone Homer did it
- Homer arrested but escapes and everyone hunts him down
- only Lisa believes he's innocent
- Mr Burns realises he's wrong – everyone is sorry
- teaches us not to believe all that we hear

Concl — every episode has a lesson for adults and kids, so agree with statement

Explain how mobile phones affect our lives.

Broad organisational plan

effect 1 (positive) – make everyday events more convenient

effect 2 (positive) – make it easier for people to phone emergency services

effect 3 (negative) – make it difficult to have privacy

effect 4 (negative) – intrude on other people's lives when you use them

More detailed plan

Intro — 55% of Australians have mobiles, many effects – some positive, some negative

para 1 — positive effect – convenience

- arranging pick ups from public transport – especially parents & kids
- meeting friends when out
- text messaging

para 2 — positive effect – emergencies

- quick reporting of road accidents
- emergencies in bush
- contacting family in emergencies

para 3 — negative effect – privacy
- people you don't want to talk to can find you
- workers can be contacted at any time
- harder to find time to get away from people

para 4 — negative effect – intrude on others
- very annoying on public transport
- interrupt movies and other performances

Concl — effects both good and bad, but likely to become even greater part of lives in future

Books as we know them will disappear in the 21st century. Discuss.

Broad organisational plan

argument for	— increasing use of the Internet for researching information
argument against	— Internet has disadvantages eg. difficulty and unreliability of information
argument against	— books commonly used for enjoyment
argument for	— paper books not good for environment
overall opinion	— we will use books less but they will not disappear

More detailed plan

Intro — books developed over time, technology advancing. Will we leave books behind?

para 1 — argument for – increasing use of the Internet for researching information
- Internet quick and efficient
- information on every topic, range of sources
- less trouble than finding information in a book

para 2 — argument against – Internet has disadvantages
- can be difficult to find information because large base
- information can be unreliable

para 3 — argument against – books commonly used for enjoyment
- been around a long time
- reading stories is old pastime
- many people prefer reading books to other pastimes
- books used for education too

para 4 — argument for – paper books not good for environment
- paper comes from trees
- deforestation
- other sources better for environment

Concl — we will use books less especially for information but they won't disappear

3 Do one detailed plan for each Key Essay Question based on your broad organisational plans from the last section. Use your own paper.

Note: In the next section, you will choose **one** of the Key Essay Questions to continue with, but doing a plan for each will help you decide which one you prefer to do.

HELP!

PAGE 101

What problems do you see in this student's plan for an essay on the future of books question (*Books as we know them will disappear in the 21st century. Discuss.*)

Here are some questions to help you:

- Is the essay plan on the general topic ie. books?
- Does it address the particular topic focus ie. whether or not books will disappear in the 21st century?
- Does it address the essay task eg. to discuss?
- Is it organised in an appropriate way for a discussion essay?
- Are there any ideas or information which are off the topic or task?
- Is it detailed enough?
- Is it easy to follow?
- Does it show the order in which ideas will be mentioned?

Essay plan

Intro — books will never disappear

1 many people love reading

2 what will they be replaced by? little electronic books or computer screens — lots of books already in computer form — Internet, cdroms, use a lot in school

3 history of printing books

4 people like reading in all sorts of places — can't use electronic stuff in bath — can use paper

5 books last a long time eg. can squash them up and bend them and they're still OK

Concl — books will never disappear

Make
a first draft

You will very rarely write a good essay in one go. It will generally take at least two drafts, and very often three or more.

However, everyone works through the drafting process differently. Some writers write a first draft, then make changes and write a second draft, make changes again and write a third draft and so on.

Some make changes as they go and may do only one draft because of this – especially if they are composing their essays on the computer rather than on paper.

Others combine both methods. They make changes as they go but still see different stages of their essays as first draft, second draft, third draft and so on.

The important thing when writing a first draft is to concentrate on getting your ideas down and not worrying too much about correctness – word choice, grammar, spelling and punctuation.

Your first draft is your chance to try out the essay plan and see how it works.

In this section we will focus on five aspects of essay writing, because you will usually have to attend to these as you write your first draft – to give your essay shape and substance. Of course you will attend to them in later drafts too – adding words to link ideas better, correcting punctuation or spelling and so on.

The five sections are:

1 Drafting the Introduction
2 Drafting the Body Paragraphs
3 Drafting the Conclusion
4 Including other people's ideas
5 Linking your ideas

We will continue to work with our three Key Essay Questions as well as the Model Essay on graffiti.

From this point on you will be asked to choose **one** of the Key Essay Questions to work on as a draft.

1 Drafting the Introduction

In Step 1, we looked briefly at the overall structure of essays. We saw that every essay needs an Introduction which tells the reader:

- what you're going to write about (the topic), and
- what you are going to say about it.

We compared an essay to a large, dense, unfamiliar forest, and an essay Introduction to a signpost and map of the area. We said that without an Introduction your reader is likely to get lost in the 'forest' of your ideas. So let's look more closely at this most important part of the essay.

A useful pattern

There is more than one way to write an Introduction but it helps to have a pattern to follow. One useful pattern is:

- one or two sentences that set the context for the essay (the **lead-in**)
- a statement on the essay question which ties the whole essay together (the **thesis statement**) *Note*: Thesis is from the ancient Greek language and means 'something set down or proposed for discussion'.
- one or two sentences which show your reader how you are going to develop this statement in the Body Paragraphs (the **preview**). If the preview tells the reader exactly what points will be mentioned it is sometimes called an **essay map**.

At your age and level of writing experience, you should be mainly focused on writing an Introduction that is clear and that 'does the job'. Using a pattern like the one above will help you to do this. As you become more experienced you can experiment a bit, and try to make your Introductions interesting as well as functional.

Most important! The Introduction contains **no detail** of your view or of the points in your essay. The details go in the Body Paragraphs.

The last thing to say is that without an Introduction, you don't really have an essay. Your Introduction is the link between the essay question and the essay. The stronger and clearer this link is, the better.

HOT TIPS!

Try out these students' ideas on writing Introductions:

I hate writing the Introduction but it helps me see where I'm going. It's like a map for me as well as my reader. I look back to it as I draft the rest of the essay.

I usually write the Introduction after I have written the Body Paragraphs. By then I know what I am talking about and can write the Introduction easily.

I write a rough Introduction first – I don't worry too much about the words – I just get it down and then start on the Body. Then I come back and make it match the Body perfectly. A few times I've spent ages getting the Introduction right, then changed my mind as I got into the essay and had to rewrite the Introduction to make it match up.

Tasks

PAGE 101

1 Here is the Introduction to the graffiti essay again. Study the labels given to each part.

Almost every week there is an article or letter in the newspaper on the subject of graffiti. Usually, the writers are complaining about	← Lead-in sentence/s
quick and careless scrawls done on public or private property. This form of graffiti should not be considered as art, but other more complex and skilful forms should be.	← Thesis statement
More advanced forms of graffiti brighten up our suburbs. These forms take great artistic skill to design and carry out. If they were recognised as art, young artists would have better opportunities to develop their skills and this would benefit the community.	← Essay map (says exactly what the main arguments will be)

2 On page 4, Task 2, you identified the main statement of view (the thesis statement) of four introductions to essays on the graffiti essay topic. Here are those Introductions again.

Read the Introductions, and:

- underline the lead-in sentence/s
- circle the thesis statement
- put an asterisk at the beginning of the preview/essay map.

Note: There may not be a lead-in or preview/essay map in each case. However, there **is** a thesis statement in each.

a Street art has been around for a very long time. People were painting on cave walls thousands of years ago. Graffiti is simply a modern version of this ancient artistic tradition. It is only because it is on the street and not in an art gallery that people are so negative towards it.

b Many of the streets in our cities have been destroyed in recent years by graffiti. Graffiti is nothing more than vandalism and should never be considered as a form of art. The costs to the individuals and to the community in general are enormous.

c Graffiti is a new form of art and should be seen as such. However, this is unlikely to happen because of prejudice in our community against youth and their interests and activities.

d Graffiti has become a very big problem in our cities and towns. Huge amounts of public money are being spent cleaning it up. There is no way that this destructive activity should ever be considered as art. It is generally very ugly and usually done simply to irritate the authorities and members of the public.

3 This Introduction does what an Introduction should, but it includes too much detail. Cross out the unnecessary parts.

Graffiti has increased dramatically in our cities and towns in recent years. Almost every wall in our suburb is now covered and every week there is a letter in the local paper from someone criticising the young people who do it. Many letter writers are very abusive about graffiti artists and very prejudiced against youth in general. I have read some letters which use words like 'scum' and 'brainless vandals'. However many make good points and are right to feel upset about how graffiti is ruining the look of our streets. Graffiti is certainly not art and should not be legalised. Most graffiti is ugly to look at and the money and effort spent in cleaning it up would be better spent elsewhere. This money could be spent providing youth and other community services.

4 In the last section, there were some detailed plans for each of the Key Essay Questions. The Introductions below were based on those plans, but each one is muddled up. Can you put the sentences in the most logical order to make a good Introduction. Write the numbers 1, 2, 3 and so on to correctly order the statements.

Remember that the most common order is:

- lead-in which gives the context
- thesis statement which directly relates to the essay question, and
- preview or essay map which indicates what is to follow in the Body.

The Simpsons

a Every episode of *The Simpsons* teaches us a moral lesson, proving that the show does more than make us laugh. ______

b *The Simpsons* is a television cartoon show that has been running for many years now. It contains five main characters, all members of the Simpson family. ______

c Three examples will demonstrate this. ______

d There is Homer, the slow-witted father, Marge, the conscientious mother and wife, Bart, the mischievous young boy, Lisa, the intelligent younger sister and Maggie, the overlooked baby of the household. ______

Mobile phones

a Most of those who don't are probably young children or people who can't afford one. ______

b It is clear then that mobile phones affect our lives in many ways. ______

c The negative effects include a decrease in privacy, and the intrusion they make on other people's lives in public spaces. ______

d Approximately 11 million Australians or 55% of the population own mobile phones. ______

e The positive effects include increased convenience in daily life and usefulness in emergencies. ______

Future of books

a It is now fair to say that we are in the computer age. ______

b Over the ages, books have developed and changed, from the times of the inkpot and quills, when all books were handwritten in Latin, to these days when thousands of books are printed at a time. ______

c As we move further forwards with technology, will we be leaving our books behind us? ______

d At this point at the beginning of the 21st century, we have come to expect that books will be there for us to read and enjoy forever. ______

e But times change, trends differ and technology advances. ______

HELP!

PAGE 102

Look at this student's Introduction on *The Simpsons* Key Essay Question. How could it be improved in the next draft?

Here are some questions to help you:

- Is there a lead-in sentence which gives you some background or context?
- Is there a thesis statement?
- Does the thesis statement clearly relate back to the question?
- Does the thesis statement clearly tell you what the writer is saying on the question?
- Is there a preview or essay map which shows you what the writer is going to say in the Body?
- Do you feel you have a good idea of what the writer will say in the Body?
- Are there any details that should not be there?
- Does the Introduction make you feel confident that the writer knows what they are talking about?

The Simpsons is a great comedy, but it is really more than that in my opinion. *The Simpsons* is a cartoon about a family of five — Homer, Marge, Bart, Lisa and Maggie. There are other characters too who all live in the town of Springfield. One important one is Mr Burns who is the boss of the nuclear energy company where Homer works. *The Simpsons* is the longest running cartoon of all time and it is not hard to see why.

WORK ON YOUR KEY ESSAY QUESTION

From this point on, you can choose to work on only **one** of the Key Essay Questions.

Make your choice now. Then draft an Introduction for your essay based on the plan you did in the last section. (Of course you can change your plan at any time.)

Use the questions above in the Help task to guide you.

Remember: For the discussion question, you do not need to give your opinion in the Introduction. Instead you pose the question or issue.

2 Drafting the Body Paragraphs

The Body Paragraphs are the 'guts' of your essay. If you have written a clear Introduction, your reader will have a good idea of the sorts of points you are going to make in the Body of your essay.

But you have to **keep on being clear**. In each paragraph, you need to write in a way that helps your reader to follow your main points and to see at all times how these points develop the main idea expressed in the Introduction.

There are six important things to remember about the essay Body:

1. Your Body Paragraphs should **match up** with your essay Introduction. If you do somethiing different from what you said you'd do in the Introduction, your reader will be confused, and you will weaken your case.
2. Don't write the Body of your essay as one big slab. **Break it up** into separate paragraphs.
3. Every paragraph should be about **one main idea only**. Every sentence in the paragraph should – in some way – relate to that idea. If they don't, they should not be there.
4. Most paragraphs have a **topic sentence** which summarises this one idea. The topic sentence tells your reader what the paragraph is about. It is usually the first sentence in the paragraph. All other sentences in the paragraph relate in some way to the topic sentence.
5. You should not just repeat the idea in the topic sentence, you should **develop it**. Every sentence in the paragraph develops and extends the idea in the topic sentence. You might give two or three examples of the idea, or give reasons for the points you are making in an argument.
6. Make your paragraphs **appropriate to** your essay purpose. For example, in an argument essay, each paragraph will be about one argument and each topic sentence will be a statement of that argument. If you are writing an essay explaining the causes of something, each paragraph may be about one cause and the topic sentence will say what that cause is.

HOT TIPS!

If your essay is good, a reader could read only the Introduction and the topic sentences, and still have a very good idea of your argument. Use this check on your own writing.

It can be a good idea to end each Body Paragraph with a sentence which clearly ties it back to the essay question. The Sample Essay on page 96 is a good example of this.

1 Look again at the body paragraphs from the graffiti essay. Notice the way that each topic sentence relates.

Lead-in hints that types of graffiti will be important to the essay argument →

Thesis statement ←

Essay map says exactly what the three main arguments will be ←

Almost every week there is an article or letter in the newspaper on the subject of graffiti. Usually, the writers are complaining about quick and careless scrawls done on public or private property. This form of graffiti should not be considered as art, but other more complex and skillful forms should be. More advanced forms of graffiti brighten up our suburbs. These forms take great artistic skill to design and carry out. If they were recognised as art, young artists would have better opportunities to develop their skills and this would benefit the community.

Topic sentence picks up the idea in lead-in that not all graffiti is the same →

It is important, first of all, to distinguish between three different types of graffiti. First, there is the 'tag' which is the stylised writing of the graffiti artist's name. Then, there is the 'throw-up' which is bigger and more time-consuming than the tag, but generally ...

Topic sentence picks up first part of essay map ←

If good graffiti is seen as art and then encouraged, it has the potential to improve the look of our streets and our transport systems. Good graffiti pieces are colourful, vibrant, and attractive. In most cases, they are far more attractive than the walls they are painted on, ...

Topic sentence picks up second part of essay map →

Real graffiti pieces require high level artistic skill to design and carry out. Pieces are usually designed to cover very large areas such as walls, and so have to be planned in detail on paper first. The designs are usually intricate and involve many colours. They are usually ...

Topic sentence picks up third part of the essay map ←

Recognising talented graffitists as artists would give them the opportunity to further develop their skills. Graffiti artists need spaces where they can develop their spray can skills without breaking the law ...

2 Underline the topic sentences in these Body Paragraphs from different student essays. *Remember*: They are usually but not always first in the paragraph.

a History essay
Black Americans of the 1950s and 1960s had a difficult life. They had to be segregated in public places such as cafeterias and public transport. They were not allowed to go into non-coloured shops and they could only travel in black-owned taxis. They were not allowed to be sitting down on a bus while a white person was standing. If they were, they would be arrested. One famous incident relating to this was in 1955 when a black woman, Rosa Parks, refused to give up her seat on the bus. She was arrested and convicted by an all-white jury.

b Health essay
The thinning of the ozone layer is being caused by a family of gases discovered about 50 years ago called chlorofluorocarbons (CFCs). CFCs have been used in many everyday things such as pressurised spray cans, refrigerators and air conditioners. When the CFCs are used they slowly float up to the ozone layer. When they get there, they break down and destroy the ozone gas by converting it to oxygen. This process make take many years but eventually it thins out the ozone layer.

c Geography essay

There are three types of volcanoes. Firstly, there are active volcanoes which erupt regularly. Secondly, there are dormant volcanoes which have not erupted for a long time. Lastly, there are extinct volcanoes which have not once erupted in recorded history.

d English essay

Frost's poem "The Road Not Taken" appears at first to be about a traveller who takes one path over another. But looking more deeply it is really about the decisions and choices a traveller in life often faces. Frost seems to be saying that the traveller who faces the choice of two paths in life and takes the one that appears to be less well travelled will be better off than those choosing the more obvious path. "The Road Not Taken" is one of the best examples of Frost's gentle symbolism.

e Physical Education essay

The physical attributes needed for a sprinter are different from those required for a marathon runner. Sprinters need great strength. Because of this, they have very well developed arm and leg muscles. Their bodies look solid and powerful. Long distance runners, on the other hand, need stamina more than strength. They tend to be extremely thin and may even look weak. As well as stamina, they need a very strong will because a long distance event is a test of the mind as well as the body.

3 Look again at the paragraphs above and at the way the writers have developed the idea in the topic sentences. Match the paragraphs to the methods of development below.

i gives examples ______

ii compares and contrasts two things ______

iii gives reasons to support a statement ______

iv gives more detail to explain something ______

v describes different categories of a thing ______

4 Underline the sentence in each of the paragraphs below which does not relate to the idea in the topic sentence.

a History essay

There is evidence suggesting that Neanderthal man believed in an afterlife. The bodies found in graves were in the foetal position which could symbolise some belief in a rebirth after death. Also the heads were covered with a stone slab which may have been because the Neanderthals thought it gave protection to the deceased. They obviously had the ability to think and solve problems and work together. Some bodies were found with a joint of meat placed in the grave, which may indicate a belief that the spirit needed something to sustain them on a journey into some kind of afterlife.

b English essay

Romeo and Juliet's parents bear some of the responsibility for the lovers' deaths. Their stubbornness about the ancient grudge between their families was the main cause for the secrecy of Romeo and Juliet's love. If the two were able to love each other openly, they would not have had to resort to Friar Lawrence's plan and therefore they would not have died. The nurse had some responsibility because she brought the two together.

5 Match the topic sentences (**a**, **b** and **c**) to the paragraphs below from one student's essay on ancient Greece.

a There is some doubt about the original purpose of the ancient Olympic Games.

b The procedures and practices of the ancient Olympic Games were different to the modern Olympic Games.

c One source that tells us that the ancient Olympic Games were significant was the Olympic Truce.

i ______

The Truce, discovered by archaeologists, was written around the rim of a discus. The terms of the truce were that warfare was stopped during the games. Also it was forbidden to carry on a court case and to execute criminals. If you broke the truce, you were heavily fined.

ii ______

It is possible that they were held to keep men fit for fighting. Events like the javelin and racing in armour were certainly based on military skills, although other events were simply tests of athletic ability. It is also clear from written records that another major purpose was religious – to honour Zeus.

iii ______

The program included such things as oaths to Zeus, sacrifices to Pelops, chariot races, and a boys' competition. Instead of getting medals, the winners received wreaths made from a branch of the sacred olive tree and wore victory ribbons around their arms, legs and head. The spectators came from all over the Greek world – on foot, donkey or by boat. When they arrived they stayed for the whole festival, and unless they were very important and rich, camped in tents or just on the ground.

6 This student had good ideas in his history essay on knights and weaponry. However, he has not divided them up into separate paragraphs. Can you mark where the paragraphs should start and finish? (There are four paragraphs.)

Knights were very important in medieval England. They rode on warhorses into battle and made up the cavalry. Each knight had his own squire. This was a young boy who was in training to be a knight. The squire helped him to put on his extremely expensive armour and helped saddle the warhorse which was also extremely expensive. A warhorse would cost around 85 pounds — an amount that would take an ordinary foot soldier 32 years to earn. The weapons for the knights stayed basically the same all through the Middle Ages. The most important was the sword. Although the design of the sword changed throughout the Middle Ages, the basis of the design stayed the same – consisting of a hilt (or handle), two quillions (cross guards) and a pommel (a heavy round weight to balance the sword). Swords were very highly valued. They were generally secured to the knight's breast by a long chain so they would not be lost in battles. The hilt was sometimes studded with jewels and the pommel was sometimes filled with precious things such as the remains of a holy person. Knights also fought with a lance, a kind of long spear that could reach up to fifteen feet in length. The lance was made of wood and either had a fire-hardened tip or a steel cap. Knights would either throw the lance like a javelin or charge during battle and try to knock the other knight off his horse.

HELP!

PAGE 102

Look at this paragraph on *The Future of Books* Key Essay Question. How could it be improved in the next draft?

Here are some questions to help you:

- Is there only one main idea?
- Is there a topic sentence which states this main idea?
- Is the topic sentence clear?
- Does the writer develop the topic sentence or just repeat the one idea?
- Does the writer develop it in an appropriate way for the essay purpose?

Books are very portable. You can take them everywhere. You can take them to the beach, on the bus or train, and you can take them to bed. You might be able to do this with an electronic book but it would not be the same. Besides, most people like the feel of books. They like turning the pages and they even like stroking the covers and pictures. Children especially like doing this with their picture books. On the other hand electronic books are portable too so perhaps there is not much difference.

WORK ON YOUR KEY ESSAY QUESTION

Draft the Body Paragraphs for the Key Essay Question you are working on, using your plan and your Introduction as your guide.

Don't worry about getting everything right. Remember it is only a draft.

Use the questions above in the Help task to guide you in your draft.

3 Drafting the Conclusion

In Step 1, we said that every essay needs a conclusion to remind the reader of the 'journey' through the 'forest' of ideas. The Conclusion reminds your reader of:

- why you wrote the essay
- what you wrote in it, and
- what your main idea was throughout the essay.

It can be hard to think of a Conclusion when you are at the end of your essay. Most people would agree with this student:

> *I **hate** writing the Conclusion. I usually just want to finish by the time I get there. It's hard to think of a different way to say what I have said already. Sometimes I end up just repeating the Introduction.*

Why important?

The Conclusion **is** worth doing well. If your reader lost track during your essay, the Conclusion gives them a final chance to get back on track and understand your essay. Because it is the last thing your reader reads, it is very, very important. A good Conclusion can even make your reader forget some of the not-so-good parts in the essay Body.

A useful pattern

There is no single way to write Conclusions, and it depends very much on the type of essay question. However, a good pattern to follow is:

- summarise the main points of your Body Paragraphs – in a general way or point-by-point (like a mirror of your preview/essay map in the Introduction)
- state or restate your point of view on the topic
- round off the essay in some way with a final comment or statement.

Most important!

- Do **not** introduce any new points or examples in the Conclusion. Only refer to what you have already written.
- Do **not** include any detail. The Conclusion – like the Introduction – is for main ideas only.
- Make sure your Conclusion matches up with your Introduction, but try to avoid using exactly the same words that you used there.

Finally, if you don't have an essay Conclusion, you don't have an essay. If your Conclusion is clear and strong, it shows that you really do believe what you have written, and this makes your essay more convincing.

HOT TIP!

After you draft your Conclusion, always:

- **re-read the essay question to see that you have answered it**
- **re-read your Introduction to see that it 'matches' your Conclusion.**

Tasks

PAGE 102

1 Here is the Conclusion of the graffiti essay showing the way it picks up the ideas in the topic sentences of the Body Paragraphs.

It is important, first of all, to distinguish between three different types of graffiti ... ← *Topic sentence*

If good graffiti is seen as art and then encouraged, it has the potential to improve the look of our streets and our transport systems ... ← *Topic sentence*

Real graffiti pieces require high level artistic skill to design and carry out ... ← *Topic sentence*

Recognising talented graffitists as artists would give them the opportunity to further develop their skills ... ← *Topic sentence*

To sum up, there is more than one kind of graffiti. The more basic forms are generally not art. However, the more complex examples of graffiti are a form of art requiring considerable artistic skill. If these forms of graffiti were recognised as art, they could make our streets more attractive and, at the same time, give talented young artists an opportunity to develop their skills further and contribute their creative skills to their community.

Summary of points – taken from topic sentences →

← *Restatement of thesis statement* (However, the more complex examples of graffiti are a form of art requiring considerable artistic skill.)

(no rounding off comment in this Conclusion)

2 In the left column below are three Introductions (A–C). In the right column are the matching Conclusions (i–iii).

a Match the Introductions to the Conclusions.

b Underline the words in the Conclusions that express the words underlined in the Introductions in a different way.

Introductions	Conclusions
A. Street art has been around for a very long time. People were painting on cave walls thousands of years ago. Graffiti is simply a modern version of this ancient artistic tradition. It is only because it is on the street and not in an art gallery that people are so negative towards it.	i. While older people hold onto their stereotypical views of youth, graffiti will never be seen as art. Youth and community workers should, however, be working to change these views. If they do, perhaps one day graffiti will take its place as a legitimate form of art.
B. Many of the streets in our cities have been destroyed in recent years by graffiti. Graffiti is nothing more than vandalism and should never be considered as a form of art. The costs to the individual's and to the community in general are enormous.	ii. Graffiti is no different from the wall drawings and paintings that have been done from the beginning of man's time on Earth. While not everyone may like it, it is a form of artistic expression and should not be illegal.
C. Graffiti is a new form of art and should be seen as such. However, this is unlikely to happen because of prejudice in our community against youth and their interests and activities.	iii. Graffiti is not art. It is simply destruction of public and private property. If the people who carry out this vandalism are made to clear it up, then we might not see so much of it in the future.

3 Look at these Conclusions (A-D).

a Circle the type of essay question the student was answering from one of those below:

discuss   argue   explain   compare /contrast

b Underline any words used to indicate that the paragraph is a conclusion, for example:

overall   to sum up   in conclusion   to conclude   in the end   on the whole

Conclusion A

Overall the positive and negative effects of TV viewing balance out. If we watch TV in moderation and choose good programs then we can learn from it and enjoy it. However, if we let TV rule our lives, it can harm us mentally and physically, and then we should seriously think about throwing our sets away.

Conclusion B

Written records, decorated vases, sculptures and paintings uncovered by archaeologists have told us a great deal about the ancient Olympic Games. Now, over 2000 years later, we know about the purpose, the events, the procedures and the practices of the Games. As well as that, we know how important the Games were to the people of ancient Greece.

Conclusion C

To conclude, life at the turn of the last century was very different from now. Transport, communication and housing are only three of the very many areas in which our ancestors' lives were more difficult and more isolated than ours today. No doubt, in one hundred years time, people might say the same thing about life at the turn of this century.

Conclusion D

To sum up, there is no good reason to wear school uniforms. They are expensive, uncomfortable and usually unattractive. While they might be a valued school tradition for many schools, all schools should think seriously about abandoning this tradition for practical reasons.

4 This Conclusion from a History essay does what a Conclusion should, but it includes a lot of unnecessary detail. Cross out the parts you think seem too detailed.

Though aspects of the Celtic life style may seem barbaric to us, such as human sacrifices, the displaying of decapitated heads and going to war naked, we should not place our twentieth century standards onto these people from a very different time. Most evidence portrays the Celts as a highly civilised people compared to other cultures of the time, for example the equality of women, religious practices and astronomy, the skills in metal work and art and the immense respect for bards and Druids, and the fact that rulers could be elected. No matter how barbaric the Celts were in battle, they were an educated, caring and clean society as a whole and in many ways were more civilised than the society we now live in, particularly in their respect for their natural environment.

HELP!

PAGE 102

In the Help! box of the Introduction section, you looked at an Introduction on the *Simpsons* question. Here is that Introduction again:

The Simpsons is a great comedy, but it is really more than that in my opinion. *The Simpsons* is a cartoon about a family of five – Homer, Marge, Bart, Lisa and Maggie. There are other characters too who all live in the town of Springfield. One important one is Mr Burns who is the boss of the nuclear energy company where Homer works. *The Simpsons* is the longest running cartoon of all time and it is not hard to see why.

Now look at the Conclusion to that essay. How could it be improved in the next draft?

Here are some questions to help you:

- Is there a clear statement or restatement of the essay question?
- Does there appear to be a summary of ideas referred to in the essay Body? (You can't know this for sure.)
- Does the Conclusion appear to include any new or detailed points? (Again, you can't know this for sure.)
- Does it match the Introduction in some way?
- Does it round off the essay in some way?
- Does the writer use different words from the Introduction?

The Simpsons does more than make us laugh. It is however very, very funny. In my opinion, Homer is the funniest member of the family especially in the episodes involving food. However, he is also the saddest. This is one of the ways that it does more than make us laugh. If we just thought the characters were funny it would be a straight comedy, but because we can see the other side to them, it proves that the show is more complicated. *The Simpsons* would not have run for so long if it had just been a comedy.

WORK ON YOUR KEY ESSAY QUESTION

Draft a Conclusion for your essay.

Use the questions in the Help task above to guide you.

In your summary of your points, use some words from the topic sentences of your paragraphs but don't write them out completely.

Use one of these phrases to begin your conclusion:

To sum up	*In conclusion*	*To conclude*
Overall	*In the end*	*On the whole*

4 Including other people's ideas

At some point in your essay, you will probably need to use the ideas of other people that you have found in books, encyclopaedias, or on Internet sites.

When you do this you need to **either**:

- quote the person's words exactly and use quotation marks to show that you have done this, **or**
- put the person's ideas into your own words.

If you write exactly what someone else has written it and pretend it is your own wording, it is usually very obvious. The unusual words and complicated sentence structures usually give it away!

Putting someone's else's writing into your own words and keeping the meaning the same is called **paraphrasing**.

Students don't always accept the need to paraphrase. They say:

Why should I change their words? The people who write books are much better writers than me and they're experts on the subject. Isn't it better to use their words?

Well, while it is perfectly OK to have some quotations in your essay, it is good to mix them with paraphrases. If your essay is chock-a-block with quotations strung together with a few words from you, your teacher won't be able to see if you have understood what you have read. Your essay will also be quite hard to follow.

Sometimes you will have to **summarise** someone else's writing as well as paraphrase. It is not a good idea to use very big slabs of quotations in your essay. It is better to pick out the main ideas and interesting or important details and then put the whole thing into your own words, with perhaps just one sentence quoted.

Important: Whether you directly quote what someone has written, or put it into your own words, you will need to say where you got the information from. This is called **referencing**, and is dealt with in Step 4, Section 3: *Referencing your work*.

HOT TIP!

A good way to avoid the temptation of copying big slabs of text into your essay is to take notes first and then write the text from your notes.

Tasks

PAGE 103

1 Look at this example of a paraphrase from the Model Essay. Take notice of the different ways the essay writer changes the words.

Original text		Paraphrased text
The sad thing is that because of the aspect of <u>vandalism</u> usually associated with graffiti, the art is often quite temporary and can be gone within minutes. A piece that may be 50 feet long and <u>10 feet high</u> and has taken at least 8 hours and up to 30 cans of paint ~~can be painted~~ over in just minutes. (taken from Tucker, D. O. *Graffiti*: <u>Art and Crime</u> (online) http://www-atdp-berkeley.edu/Studentpages/cflores/historygraffiti.html p. 5.)	• same words • words left out • extra words but no change to meaning • detail left out • different sentence structure overall	However, because graffiti is usually seen as <u>vandalism</u>, no matter what the works look like, they are usually painted over in dull colours. (Tucker, online p. 5)

2 Put these texts on the three Key Essay Questions into your own words. Make sure you keep the meaning the same. Two suggestions for how you could begin your paraphrase are beneath each paragraph.

a (*Future of books*)

For electronic books to be accepted by the general population, they would need to come up with a page-turning mechanism of some kind. Turning the page is just so much part of the book experience for most people, especially when reading novels. We even have a word which reflects our liking for this experience. We call books that are very exciting and pleasurable to read 'page - turners'.

Electronic books would have to have ...

One thing people like about books is ...

____

____

____

____

____

b (*Mobile phones*)

Most people would admit that there is a need to block the use of their phones at times. They would probably not object to an external device which, for example, automatically turned off everyone's phones as they entered a movie theatre or an aeroplane. Such a device would create real mobile-free areas. Peace and safety would not be then dependent on individuals.

There are some places that mobile phones simply ...

Although most people turn off their phones in places like ...

____

____

____

____

____

b (*Simpsons*)

The secret of *The Simpsons* success may be that it appeals to all ages. Children enjoy the obvious humour and physical jokes. Adults enjoy the more subtle and sometimes quite dark humour. Adults are also more likely than children to pick up the moral issues dealt with.

Both adults and children ...

Adults probably watch *The Simpsons* in a different way ...

____

____

____

____

____

3 Look at this example of a summary from an essay on the graffiti topic. Take notice of the way the essay writer picks up the main ideas and leaves out the detail.

Original text		Summarised version
There are many different styles and ways of saying what a certain type of graffiti is. Many people create names for their own styles and some are involved in things that are completely original and can't be defined. However, there are <u>three main and distinct levels and types of graffiti</u> that are produced by graffitists. <u>First, there's the 'tag' – the stylised writing of a name.</u> Following the tag <u>is the 'throw-up' which is a quickly done type of graffiti that is more time consuming and much bigger than most tags.</u> Throw-ups usually are made of <u>bubble letters</u> and are no more than <u>two colors</u>. *Subway Art* says a throw-up is 'a name painted quickly with one layer of spray paint and an outline.' After the throw-up, <u>there's the more complex and more skilful 'piece' (short for masterpiece) or 'burner'.</u> The <u>ability</u> to do pieces and burners is where the term 'graffiti artists' most appropriately comes into play. Although tags and throw-ups can be very well executed and have great style, it is the piece work that allows a graffitist to really show everyone what he/she is about. (taken from Tucker, D. O. *Graffiti: Art and Crime* (online) http://www-atdp-berkeley.edu/Studentpages/cflores/historygraffiti.html p. 3.)	main ideas only most detail left out	... three different types of graffiti. First, there is the 'tag' which is the stylised writing of the graffiti artist's name. Then, there is the 'throw-up' which is bigger and more time-consuming than the tag, but generally just big bubble letters in two colours. Lastly, there is the 'piece' (short for 'masterpiece') which takes considerable skill and time to execute. (Tucker, online, p. 3)

4 Summarise the following text on the effects of TV watching. Here are some possible ways to begin:
There is no agreement about the effects that TV viewing has on children ...
Research gives us differing views on the effect of TV viewing on children ...
There is no clear evidence either way about the effect of TV viewing on children ...

Note: Don't worry in this exercise about including the names of the studies and the references.

Children and TV

Research results give conflicting results about the effects of television on children. Some research suggests there is no problem at all in children watching hours and hours of television each day. One study, for example, found that children watch TV actively, taking note of the things they are interested in and turning to other things when they are not interested (Ho, 1999). It showed that children simply do not sit in front of shows that bore them. This research suggested that children have perhaps becoming more discriminating and critical of what they watch since TV was first invented.

Other studies suggest that they do not generally watch as much as is often thought, and that usually they do not watch unsuitable programs. A nationwide study by the Australian Broadcasting Authority and Office of Film and Literature Classification (Chan, 1996) recently showed that most parents set strict rules for their children so that they do not in fact watch hours upon hours. Seventy five percent of parents in this study believed that their children had a good balance between TV watching and other activities. Parents mostly supervised what children watched especially if they were under eight years of age.

However, other studies raise fears that children are watching too much television and that it is not good for them. For example, a study by the Australasian College of Physicians found that toddlers are watching TV for up to two and a half hours a day. By 30 months, children are 'glued to the box' for an average of 84 minutes a day rising to two and a half hours by the time the child is four (Kelly & Pash, 1999, p.3). This much TV at this important stage of physical and mental development was thought to be very damaging.

What is more, a South Australian study found that one in ten children spends more time watching television than attending school (*Sydney Morning Herald*, 2001, p.3). Ten per cent of the children surveyed in this study spent more than 1000 hours in front of the television set in one year. Equally alarmingly, the study also found the average hours that children watched each year was 630 hours which was more than half the time the children spent in school.

Television has also been blamed for increasing consumption of junk food in a University of Tasmania and Deakin University research study (Darby, 1998). This study found that the more hours a day that teenagers watched TV, the more junk food such as soft drink, meat pies and hot chips they ate.

WORK ON YOUR KEY ESSAY QUESTION

Look at the stimulus texts on the Key Essay Questions in the Extras section. If you have used parts of these texts in your draft, check to see:

- if you have paraphrased not plagiarised
- if your summaries have expressed the main idea of the original text
- if you need any quotation marks for parts you have taken exactly from the text.

If you have not included any parts of these texts, try to do so now.

5 Making your essay 'hang together'

We have talked about the importance of keeping your reader with you – of helping him or her to keep track of your one main idea and how you are developing it.

One of the very important aspects of doing this is something called **cohesion**. This refers to the wholeness or the one-ness of a piece of writing. Cohesion is about your essay 'hanging together'.

If your reader can easily follow your ideas throughout your essay and clearly see that it is all of one piece, then your essay has cohesion. If your reader does not, and instead sees it as a series of disconnected sentences, then your writing lacks cohesion.

When you are reading a text which lacks cohesion, you constantly have to read back over what you have read. You think "Why is he telling me this now?" or "What's the connection here?" When you read a text which has cohesion, you don't even notice you are reading. One sentence seems to flow into the next.

Difference between speaking and writing

Cohesion is something that does not matter so much in conversation. We often ramble in conversation, talking about things in a confusing order or stopping and starting and so on. But in conversation the listener can ask the speaker to repeat or clarify things. The listener can also use the situation to work out any confusing bits of the conversation.

The reader does not have this luxury. There are only the words on the page and you are not there to help make the connection between your ideas clear. You are not there to say "Oh yeah I am talking again about that idea I mentioned a few sentences ago". Your writing has to say all this by itself and say it clearly.

How to make your writing cohesive

To make your writing cohesive you:

- repeat key content words or use words with similar meaning through the text
- use words like *it, this, these, that, those, there, such,* and *other* (usually pronouns) to refer to things mentioned in other parts of the text
- use words like *therefore, in fact, however, furthermore, on the other hand* and so on to link ideas in different sentences (sometimes called connectors)
- use words like *although, whereas, if, unless, after, when* to link ideas within the same sentence (conjunctions)
- order the information in your sentences in a way that makes it easy for the reader to see the connections between them.

It does not matter how good the information and ideas are in your essay, if you aren't able to combine them into a good text then you will lose your reader.

HOT TIP!

Try to put yourself in the place of your reader. After you write each paragraph, read it over to see if it all 'connects'. Then look back at the previous paragraph, and see if it connects to that also.

Tasks

PAGE 103

1 Look at this paragraph from the Model Essay on graffiti, and take notice of the techniques used to make the text cohesive.

Repetition of key content words, or use of similar words

Ordering of information

> If good graffiti is seen as art and then encouraged, it has the potential to improve the look of our streets and our transport systems. Good graffiti pieces are colourful, vibrant, and attractive. In most cases, they are far more attractive than the walls they are painted on, which in the old parts of cities are often ugly, dull and uncared for. There are many examples of spectacular murals in the inner city. In fact some have even become tourist attractions. There are also excellent examples of graffiti on passenger or freight trains. However, because graffiti is usually seen as vandalism, no matter what the works look like, they are usually painted over in dull colours (Tucker, online p. 5).

Pronouns referring back to things already mentioned

Words linking ideas in different sentences

Words linking ideas in the same sentence

Now look at the way the ideas are ordered in that paragraph. You will see the way the writer often begins a sentence with an idea already mentioned – usually in the previous sentence. This is an important aspect of cohesion.

Information already mentioned	New information
If good graffiti is seen as art, it	has the potential to improve the look of our streets and our transport systems.
Good graffiti pieces	are colourful, vibrant, and attractive.
In most cases, they	are far more attractive than the walls ...
There	are many examples of spectacular murals ...
In fact some	have even become tourist attractions.
There	are also excellent examples of graffiti on passenger or freight trains.
However, because graffiti is usually seen as vandalism ... they	are usually painted over in dull colours.

2 Here are some words used to connect information and ideas across two sentences. Try to use them more in your essay writing.

Adding information or ideas	Showing cause or result	Saying in another way or giving examples	Showing time	Showing the sequence of ideas	Contrasting ideas or talking about conditions
too also in addition furthermore what's more on top of that besides likewise apart from that as well	so therefore then consequently for this reason because of this as a result due to this	for example for instance that is in fact in other words in particular namely	then next afterwards until then at the same time meanwhile previously later eventually	firstly secondly first of all finally to sum up to conclude to start with overall in conclusion	however nevertheless despite this on the other hand in contrast instead yet otherwise

3 Choose the best connector to use between the sentences below on the future of books Key Essay Question.

for example   nevertheless   furthermore   for this reason   eventually   in the first place

a It is difficult to imagine reading a book that is not made of paper. ______________ most people eventually adjust to changes that we cannot imagine.

b Basically, books look and feel better than electronic books. ______________ it is unlikely that they will ever be completely replaced by them.

c There are numerous advantages in electronic books. ______________, they will be able to hold so much more information than a regular sized book.

d Electronic book forms are already replacing large information texts such as encyclopaedias. ______________ they will probably also replace fiction.

e Reading a book on a computer screen is not the most comfortable thing to do. ______________ you can only do it in a room that has a computer.

f There are many reasons why paper based books will never disappear. ______________ only the rich have access to computer technology.

4 Read the following History essay extract (about early humans), taking particular notice of the underlined words and what they refer to. Then answer the questions below.

The first tools were made by *Homo habilis* or 'handy man', who is known as the earliest human being. Using their ability to solve problems, these people crafted many items to make their lives easier. These gave them access to a more varied diet. *Homo erectus* or 'upright man', created more elaborate tools which were crafted out of flint. These people also made weapons out of stone, animal hide and wood. However the most sophisticated tools were manufactured by the *Homo sapiens* or 'intelligent man'. This group invented very finely crafted tools. What made their tools and weapons so remarkable was the attention to detail and the accuracy of each piece to serve its set purpose. *Homo sapiens* also set stone into wooden bases to make spears and knives. Such achievements would have taken great skill.

Homo sapiens also created art. This was mainly rock wall art although their earliest art was portable art – sculptures, engravings and personal adornments. The paintings often depicted the killing of animals in the hunt. The purpose of the paintings is not certain. One theory is that they had some religious or spiritual purpose, because they were often found in large caves probably used for rituals and ceremonies. These rituals would have helped to bind and strengthen the community. Another theory is that they were to bring luck to a hunt – painting the animals would make it more likely that they would catch them.

a ... these people crafted many items to make their lives easier. Which people? ____________________

b These gave them access to a more varied diet. What gave them access? ____________________

c ... created more elaborate tools which were crafted out of flint. More elaborate than what? ____________________

d This group invented very finely crafted tools. Which group? ____________________

e Such achievements would have taken great skill. What sort of achievements? ____________________

f ... their earliest art was portable art. Whose art? ____________________

g The paintings often depicted the killing. Which paintings? ____________________

h One theory is that they had some religious or spiritual purpose. One theory about what? ____________________

i These rituals would have helped to bind and strengthen the community. What rituals? ____________________

j Another theory is that they were to bring luck to a hunt. Theory about what? ____________________

5 Sequence the paragraph below. Use the words in italics to help you.

a The black population of America attempted to change *this*. ______

b *Despite this*, there is still racial inequality in the USA today. ______

c *Since that time*, the attitudes of white people towards black people has changed significantly and this has been due in a large way to the efforts of King and other leaders of the civil rights movement. ______

d In the United States of America in the 1950s and 1960s, African-Americans had very few rights. ______

e *They* were led by perhaps the most important black individual of our time, Martin Luther King. ______

6 Do the same for this paragraph.

a *They* can also help memory, because to play *the* games you have to remember complicated commands. ______

b While games have been criticised for promoting violence, *the* manufacturers say the market has now moved away from war games to educational games. ______

c Video game manufacturers say that games can be important learning tools. ______

d *They* can improve hand-to-eye co-ordination and sharpen reflexes. ______

e *These* simulate real-life experiences such as driving cars or flying planes. ______

HELP!

PAGE 103

Look at this paragraph on the future of books. Can you help to make it more cohesive?

Here are some questions to help you:

- Do you need to repeat or change some words to make it easier to follow the ideas?
- Can you add any reference words like *this, these, it, they*?
- Can you add some linking words between sentences eg. *however, as a result*?
- Can you link up some sentences to make one sentence eg. with *and* or *but*?
- Would re-ordering the words in any sentences make the paragraph easier to read?

It is difficult for many people to imagine a world where there will be more electronic books than paper books. They will not disappear. Computer texts will be used alongside books. There will be more and more information texts placed on computer. Most encyclopaedias are already on computer. Many encyclopaedia companies no longer publish print versions.

WORK ON YOUR KEY ESSAY QUESTION

Look back over your essay draft. Check to see if you need to improve the way it 'hangs together', using some of the techniques in this section.

Use the questions in the Help task above to guide you.

STEP FOUR

Revise and polish

Very few people can put down the pen at the end of one draft of an essay, and feel confident it is good enough. Most of us need to read it over again carefully, and attend to different points of structure and language. We need to **revise** and **polish** our writing.

In fact most of us need to do this a lot more than once for an important essay. The one time when we have no choice but to do it all in one go is in examinations.

In this Step we will look at five aspects of revising and polishing your writing. Of course in reality you will be attending to these aspects as you draft as well, but you will be leaving the fine-tuning to this revision stage.

It is also true that you will be attending in this stage to some of the aspects of essay writing we have already talked about in Step 3. You will, for example, be making sure your Introduction really does introduce your essay and sets up your reader's expectations of what is to follow. You will be checking again to see if your paragraphs are really about one idea only. You will be adding some linking words or changing the word order to make sure that your essay 'hangs together', and so on.

The five aspects dealt with in this Step are:

1 Writing grammatical sentences
2 Using the right kind of language
3 Referencing your work
4 Using good spelling strategies
5 Getting the punctuation right.

You should continue to work on your Key Essay Question throughout this Step, checking the aspects mentioned in each section.

1 Writing grammatical sentences

Having a good overall structure for your essay is very important. It can often make up for mistakes in language. Your reader forgives or sometimes does not even notice your grammar mistakes, because he or she can follow your line of thought from paragraph to paragraph quite well.

However it **is** very important to have grammatically correct sentences too. You might wonder why teachers make such a fuss about good grammar. Well, they do it for a good reason.

Why important?

Grammar helps you make your meaning clear. Grammar is **not** just a bunch of rules set down by somebody to trip you up and confuse you. Grammar is what makes our language work. It is the main reason we can understand each other when we talk or write.

When you think about how complex our ideas often are, it is truly amazing that we communicate at all. Just remember, we have grammar to thank for this achievement.

Difference between essays and other types of writing

In formal academic writing such as essays, you must write good, complete sentences. This suits your writing purpose.

In some types of writing complete sentences are not so important. In fact, writers play with sentence structures for particular effects. When writing a story, for example, it is perfectly OK to write the following:
The principal comes around the corner. My heart beats. Ka-boom ka-boom. Loud as a drum. Surely she will hear it.
The underlined words are not sentences and so would not be acceptable in an essay.

You even see this sort of writing in quite serious newspaper articles. Be on the lookout for it but don't try to copy it in your essays.

It is not possible here to cover every single bit of grammar that is important for essay writing. That would take another whole book. So, we will just provide some very basic guidance about sentence structure – about what **is** and what **is not** a sentence.

We will also give you a few tips to help you put together a good sentence and to avoid some very common mistakes.

HOT TIP!

If you are working on a computer, the grammar check CAN be a useful aid. If you take time to think about the corrections, you can learn from your mistakes. However, it can be overwhelming and distracting from your thought processes when your whole page is underlined with squiggly lines. Also the grammar check is not completely reliable, so you really need to develop your own sense of what is correct and what is not, instead of relying on the computer grammar check.

Tasks

PAGES 103 – 104

Simple sentences

- A **sentence** is a group of words that express a complete thought.
- A sentence must have a complete verb (eg. *see, thinks, have decided*).
- Most sentences also have a noun (eg. *people, democracy*), a pronoun (eg. *he, they*), or a noun group (eg. *thousands of people*) which is the subject of the sentence – what the sentence is all about.
- **Simple sentences** contain only one unit of meaning, called a **clause**.
- The simplest sentences contain only a subject and a verb. For example:
  The people voted. *Democracy flourished.*
- Most simple sentences also contain other information after the subject and verb, for example:
  The people voted for a new leader. *Democracy flourished under his rule.*
- Sentences which give commands or instructions sometimes consist of a verb only (eg. *Go! Stop!*) because the subject (*you*) is understood.
- A common mistake is thinking that a group of words with only a part-verb is a sentence.
  Having seen the results. (**not** a sentence) *They saw the results.* (a sentence)
  Being a good man. (**not** a sentence) *He is a good man.* (a sentence)

1 Underline the sentence subject and circle the verb in these simple sentences.

a *The Simpsons* has been running for more than 10 years.

b Paper books have a future.

c Mobile phones are being used for many everyday purposes.

d Graffiti has a bad name.

e Most television cartoons aim only to entertain.

f Computer technology is being updated constantly.

2 Write **S** next to the sentences below. Write **NS** if they are not sentences. If they are not, rewrite them as sentences in the space below

For example, *Being better for large amounts of information*. (This is not a sentence because it contains only the -ing form of the verb. It could be changed to *Electronic books are better for large amounts of information*.)

a Having entertained people for a very long time. ________

b Older members of our society are unlikely to take up electronic ways of reading. ________

c Most graffiti artists are young men. ________

d Being first shown on American television in 1990. ________

e Many health concerns about mobile phones have no basis. ________

f Having begun in the subways of New York City. ________

____

____

____

____

Compound sentences

- Many sentences contain more than one unit of meaning (or clause).
- Some of these sentences contain clauses which are equally important. Each clause can stand alone and be understood.
- These types of sentences are called **compound sentences.**

For example:

Mobile phones take away your privacy and they can be irritating also.
Parents sometimes hate mobile phones but children usually love them.

- When the subject of the two clauses is the same, we often omit it in the second clause, eg. *Books fall apart easily and (books) are heavy to move around.*
- Where we have two clauses of equal importance we can join them with the conjunctions *and, but,* or *or.*
- If we do **not** use these conjunctions, we must use a full stop to break up the clauses into separate sentences, or use a connector such as *however, likewise, otherwise.*
- If we use connectors like *however* or others from the chart on page 60 to connect two clauses, we need a full stop at the end of the sentence.
- A common mistake is putting two equal clauses together without a full stop, or without an *and, but* or *or*:

They have been around for a long time, many people still do not like them. (**not** correct)
They have been around for a long time, however many people still do not like them. (**not** correct)
They have been around for a long time, but many people still do not like them. (correct)
They have been around for a long time. Many people still do not like them. (correct)
They have been around for a long time. However, many people still do not like them. (correct)
Note: We can separate two equal clauses with a comma, if there is a third equal clause following eg. *Books fall apart easily, they are heavy to move around and they take up a lot of space.*

3 Correct these sentences by using a full stop or by using *and, but* or *or.*

a Video games can develop children's imagination, they can also encourage violence.

____

b Video games develop problem solving skills, furthermore they require considerable concentration.

____

c Everyone has a different view on art, most people cannot be persuaded to change their minds.

____

d There are books for reading, there are books for reference.

____

e Most cartoon shows are aimed at children, however *The Simpsons* clearly targets adult viewers as well.

____

f Video games develop some very useful skills, for example, they improve reflexes.

____

g We can read books on computer screens, we can read them in hand held e-books.

____

h This show must be more than a comedy, otherwise it would not be so popular.

____

i Children are playing computer games more and more, they are watching TV less.

____

j Unfortunately most graffiti is ugly, therefore it should not be legalised.

____

Complex sentences

- Many sentences with more than one clause have
  - one clause which is the important 'stand-alone' clause (the **main** clause), and
  - another less important clause that depends for meaning on the main clause (the **dependent** clause).
- These types of sentences are called **complex sentences**. In the examples below the main clause is underlined:
  If paper books disappear completely, *many people will have no access to literature*.
  Even though Homer makes many mistakes, *he cares about his family*.
  Text-messaging is popular because it is so quiet.
- We link main clauses to dependent clauses with conjunctions such as:
  because, when, since, after, so that, if, unless, although, whereas, as soon as, until
- A common mistake is to treat a dependent clause as a complete sentence.
  Because they are too expensive. (**not** a sentence)
  Although there are many advantages. (**not** a sentence)
  However if we link them with these stand-alone clauses, they do form sentences:
  People won't buy them, because they are too expensive.
  Although there are many advantages, many older people will refuse to buy them.

4 Write **S** next to sentences and **DC** next to dependent clauses. Convert the dependent clauses to a full sentence by adding a main clause (make one up).

a Whereas young people think quite differently. ________

b Unless people understand the style of art, they will continue to hate it. ________

c Whenever you get on a train or bus or other form of public transport. ________

d As soon as new technology appears, Australians take it up enthusiastically. ________

e If adults did graffiti, the community attitude would be quite different. ________

f Because there are many reasons in favour of the new technology. ________

____

____

____

STEP 4

HELP!

A PA(

Can you correct the sentences in this paragraph on the future of books Key Essay Question wher necessary? These questions should help you:

- Are there any clauses which need separating with a full stop?
- Are there any clauses which need joining with *and*, *but* or *or*?
- Are there any sentences without a verb or with only a part-verb (look especially for *-ing* forms)?
- Are there any sentences where two main clauses are linked with a comma and a connector such a: *however, furthermore* and so on?
- Are there any sentences which are really only dependent clauses eg. beginning with *because, unless, if*

If electronic books could be made to be more like paper books, they may make books disappear. Because people like the way books look and feel. They are unlikely to rush to buy electronic books. For example, electronic books with soft covers would be a good idea, electronic books with something to turn the pages would be useful too. Making them more like a real book. The other thing that would b needed would be a long-running battery, this would mean you would not be interrupted in the midd of an exciting story because of a flat battery. Very annoying.

WORK ON YOUR KEY ESSAY QUESTION

Read through your essay draft now and look especially for the sorts of errors explained here. Concentrate only on these things. Use the questions in the Help task above to guide you.

2 Using the right kind of language

In Step 1, Section 3 we looked briefly at how writing an essay is different from everyday conversation. Let's look more closely now at this important aspect of essay writing.

Speaking

If I asked you in conversation about the uses of mobile phones you might say:
I mostly use my mobile phone to keep in touch with my friends, but I also use it to ring my mum and tell her where I am, because she gets pretty worried if I don't.

When we speak, we're usually speaking directly to someone about personal experiences and our immediate environment. This affects the words we use and the way we put them together.

We talk about specific people and experiences (eg. *I use, my mobile phone, my friends, mum*) and use everyday 'concrete' words (eg. *keep in touch, ring, pretty worried*).

We spread out the words that contain the information (eg. *use ... mobile phone ... keep in touch ... friends ... use ... ring ... mum ... tell ... pretty worried*) and link these words up with lots of little words (eg. *to ... but ... and ... where ... because ... if*). We do this because we are thinking and speaking at the same time and it is easier this way. It is also easier for the listener who has to understand the words as they fly out of our mouths with a rush.

Writing

If you were writing a sentence in an essay on the same subject, you might write:

For most young people, mobile phones are used for socialising, and for contact with parents when away from home.

When we write, we are usually more distant from the reader and from the experiences we write about. This affects the words we use and the way we put them together.

In general, especially in formal school writing, we use more general, abstract and less personal language (eg. *most young people, mobile phones are used, socialising, contact*).

We also pack in the information words more tightly (eg. *most young people ... mobile phones ... used for socialising ... contact with parents*) with fewer little connecting words. We do this because we have time to construct our sentences and make them say what we want them to in the best possible way. We expect our readers to be able to understand this denser, tighter writing because we know they can read it again and again. It will stay there in front of their eyes – at least for a while. It will not disappear into the air the way speech does. We also need to say a lot of things in a short space. If we spread out the information as we do in speech, our essays would be a lot longer.

To sum up, in everyday speech, we mostly talk about concrete, specific, personal experiences and use language which reflects this. In essays, we might make use of these experiences but we look at them from a distance. We use abstract, general and impersonal language to reflect this.

HOT TIP!

The more you read formal written language, the easier it will be for you to use it. A good place to read it is in newspapers, especially in feature or opinion articles.

STEP 4

Tasks

PAGE 104

Avoiding personal terms like *I*, *me* and *my*

- Students are often told to avoid *I*, *me* and *my*. However, many find it difficult to understand why, if essays are supposed to be about expressing their opinions, they should not say *I think ...*, *In my opinion ...*, *In my essay ...*, *As I have shown ...* and so on.
- The reason is that an essay is not a personal piece of writing. You are not trying to connect with the reader personally as you might be in a letter or a story.
- If you refer to yourself (or to the reader) it gives the impression you are trying to make this personal connection, and this interferes with your purpose – to convince the reader of your point of view or of the truth of your explanation.
- The more you refer to yourself, the more you remind your reader of you as a person. This takes away from your reader's focus on the ideas and information. As a result, your essay will appear based on a personal viewpoint rather than on careful thought.
- Try to keep yourself out of your essay – 'disappear' from the text – and let the information and ideas do the talking.
- The easiest way to do this is to leave out these personal phrases eg:
  In my opinion, graffiti is an art form. ⟶ *Graffiti is an art form.*
- You can also substitute phrases like *It appears ...*, *Many believe ...*
  I think graffiti offends many people. ⟶ *Graffiti appears to offend many people.*

Note: While you should not refer to yourself, you can refer to *we/us* and *you* in a generic way–meaning all human beings or all people in a particular situation.

1 Take out the references to the writer in these paragraphs and, if needed, change the wording.

a I see *Animal Farm* as an analogy for the Russian Revolution.

____

b I think the author, George Orwell, tried not to take sides even though he probably had his own beliefs and views.

____

c For me, Robert Frost's strength lies in his use of symbolism.

____

d In both poems I found the symbolism meaningful and full of moral value.

____

e I understood his message to be that it is more rewarding to take the less common path when making an important life decision.

____

____

Generic statements

- In essays, we usually write about people and things in a generic way. We don't write about the man who lives next door, but we do write about the community. We don't write about our grandmother, but we do write about elderly people or senior citizens.
- We might use personal knowledge or experience of these people to express our views, but we convert it to generalised statements about groups of people.

Note: Of course in some essays, especially history essays, you do talk about individuals – a king or queen, a political leader and so on.

2 Convert these sentences about individuals to generic statements that you might use in one of the Key Essay Questions. You will probably need to change some of the other words in the sentences too.

a My great-grandfather has a mobile phone.

____

b Many of my friends have lost their mobile phones and had to pay off their contracts.

____

c I prefer paper books because I have grown up with them.

____

d Every member of my family enjoys *The Simpsons*.

____

e My parents hate *The Simpsons* only because we kids love it and want to watch it every night.

____

Noun groups and nominalisations

- One way that writers pack in meanings and at the same time convert specific experiences into more general statements is by using **noun groups** and **nominalisations**.
- A noun group is a group of words around a central noun, for example (central nouns are underlined):
  an important creative <u>opportunity</u>
  one of the greatest <u>influences</u>
  moral <u>lessons</u> for young and old
  the <u>possibilities</u> of computer technology
- A nominalisation is usually a longish noun and often ends in *-ion, -ment, -ness, -ing, -ity, - ship* or a similar suffix, for example:
  socialising (keep in touch with my friends)
  contact (ring and tell where I am)
  legalisation (making something legal)
  potential (it could happen)
- Noun groups and nominalisations also help us to put the focus in our sentences on factors, events, processes and relationships instead of individual people involved in these things. For example:
  The convenience of mobile phones has attracted many consumers.
  instead of
  Because people see how convenient mobile phones are, they are buying them.

3 Read this extract from a feature article about the future of books. Underline the noun groups or nominalisations that you find. If you do not know the meanings of the words you underline, look them up in your dictionary.

E-book manufacturers are betting that changing consumer attitudes, driven by the explosion of Internet use in recent years and the ready acceptance of hand-held devices ... have created a new and sympathetic market.

The greatest obstacle to acceptance of any e-book is the "Can I take it bed with me?" syndrome. Books – even the tackiest, well-read paperback – are intimate, tactile objects as well as portable repositories for words, images and ideas, and if an e-book doesn't have an acceptable cuddle factor, most people who read for pleasure will remain bound to the analog version. (from "You got the book", Mark Butler, Feature IT magazine, *The Weekend Australian*, Nov 14-15 1998, p. 11)

4 Match the sentences below from an essay on traditional Aboriginal society (**a-e**) to the spoken language equivalents (**i-v**).

a Aboriginal art was used for religious, social and educational purposes. ______

b Aboriginal art has been acclaimed around the world for its originality and design. ______

c The diet of Aboriginal groups was greatly influenced by their location. ______

d Survival depended on their knowledge of the seasonal availability of food and water. ______

e Rules of social behaviour strongly influenced intra-family relationships. ______

i What Aboriginal people ate depended a lot on where they were living at the time.

ii There were rules which influenced the way people behaved towards other families in the group.

iii People from around the world have praised Aboriginal art because it is very original and because it has unusual and colourful designs.

iv They survived because they knew where the food and water was at different times of the year.

v Aboriginal people painted objects and bodies for religious ceremonies and social celebrations and they also painted pictures to teach and pass on traditional stories.

5 Look back at the sentences in **4 a-e** and underline the noun groups and nominalisations.

For example, *Aboriginal art was used for religious, social and educational purposes*.

Passive voice

- When we speak about experiences and actions in everyday conversation, we and our listeners are generally interested in the people (or things) that do the actions and have the experiences.
- To show this interest, we use **active voice of verbs**. For example:
  My sister uses her mobile phone for work.
- When we write essays, we are usually not so interested in the people who do the actions. We are more interested in the actions that they are involved in – the processes and events, or the people or things acted upon.
- To show this interest, we use the **passive voice of the verb**. For example:
  Books are valued in our society. (We are interested in the books and the valuing of books **not** who values them.)
  Electronic books were introduced many years ago. (We are interested in the electronic books and their introduction **not** who introduced them.)

6 Convert these sentences from the active voice to the passive voice. Begin your sentences with the words provided.

a Researchers expect the population to reach 22 million in the next few years.

The population ____________________

b People used the word 'witchcraft' to refer to worship of the Devil.

The word 'witchcraft' ____________________

c People considered witches anti-Christian, amoral members of society.

Witches ____________________

d Scientists measure biodiversity as the number of species or subspecies of plants, animals and micro-organisms.

Biodiversity ____________________

e Historians think that Greek religion dates from about the 2nd millennium BC.

Greek religion ____________________

HELP!

PAGE 104

This paragraph is more like something from a conversation than an essay. Underline the words or sentences that make it so. Rewrite the paragraph to make it more appropriate to a written essay.

Here are some questions to help you:

- Does the writer refer to herself?
- Are there any references to individual people or groups that could be made more general?
- Does the writer need to tighten up her sentences and use fewer words?
- Could she focus better on the processes, factors and so on instead of people by using nominalisations and the passive voice?

I have read that inventors are making mobile phones more and more advanced. They are making them capable of all sorts of communication. For example, the other day on the radio I heard that a government organisation is trialling using mobile phones to tell people about bushfires and storms where they live. They would get people to register their mobile numbers and then when there was a warning about a fire or storm, they would send out a text message to everyone on the register. The people in my suburb would really like this because we live in an area that has lots of bushfires.

WORK ON YOUR KEY ESSAY QUESTION

Read through your essay draft, looking especially for parts that are too 'conversational'. Think about how best to change them using some of the language techniques shown in this section.

You may need to rewrite whole paragraphs or even your whole essay to get this right.

Use the questions in the Help task above to guide you.

3 Referencing your work

When you write essays, you almost always use facts, figures and ideas from books, encyclopaedias and Internet sites.

It is **most** important to show your readers where you have done this. This is called **referencing** your work. You must reference the text you use in the text itself and at the end in a bibliography or reference list.

Why important?

Referencing is important because it:

- shows your reader that you have taken the time to do some research and not just written something 'off the top of your head'
- shows your reader where he or she could find the original information if needed.

It is considered a very big 'sin' to pretend that somebody else's ideas are your own. This is called **plagiarising**.

Believe me, if you reference your essays correctly and end your essays with beautifully clear bibliographies, your teacher will be impressed. It may even be worth extra marks! Also, if you get into good habits now, you'll avoid problems later when correct referencing matters even more – in senior high school and at college or university.

What to reference?

In general, you must reference any ideas that you 'borrow' from someone else. Sometimes, however, you might use some materials as idea prompts (eg. newspaper articles, opinion pieces on the web) and you will not need to reference them precisely.

You must also reference facts and figures. This shows that you are basing your ideas on information from experts in the field. It also shows that your information is up-to-date.

However, where facts and figures are considered 'common knowledge', you may not always have to reference them. For example, if you are writing about China and want to mention that China includes Hong Kong and Macau, you would not need to reference this, because it is a well-known fact. You will have to decide for yourself or ask your teacher whether or not to reference facts and figures in this sort of situation.

A word of warning! Teachers can usually recognise when you have plagiarised. Firstly, they often know the book or website that you got your ideas from. Secondly, if you have copied a lot of text that someone else has written, they can usually tell the difference between your usual writing style and that of an adult expert.

HOT TIPS!

Always make a note of the *full* reference for any book or website you use as soon as you use it. This avoids the problem of returning the book to the library or turning off the Internet and then forgetting where you got the information from.

Don't leave your bibliography till last. Putting together a bibliography late at night when the essay is due at 9 o'clock the next day is not a lot of fun. So do it early – perhaps when you need a break from real writing and thinking.

Tasks

PAGE 105

Bibliography

- A bibliography is an alphabetical list of all the texts you used to write your essay.
- There are different rules for different sorts of texts, for example, books, articles, websites and so on, but in every case, you need to give enough information for your reader to find the source.
- For a book, this means: the author's name, the date of publication, the name of the text, the publisher and the place of publication.
- For example, if you wanted to include this book in your bibliography, you would write:
  Brown, K. (2002) *Essay Writing Step-by-Step*, Pascal Press, Sydney.
  Look back now at the title page and the imprint (usually second) page of this book and see where this information came from.
- Here are some examples to follow for other types of texts:
  - a later edition of a book:
    Sands, K. & Jackson, L. (2001) *Art History*, 2nd ed., Fredricks Publishing, London.
  - an article in a journal:
    Knox, J., Hill, V., & Ward, R. (2002) "The future of e-books" in *Technology Today Journal*, vol 14, no. 3, pp 23-30.
  - a newspaper article:
    Fox, H. (2001) "Boom in text messaging" in *Eastern Gazette*, 20 February, p. 34.
  - video or movie:
    Moving with the times (video recording), 25 June 2000, Spring Films.
  - website:
    What causes stormwater pollution? (online) http://www.epa.nsw.gov.au/stormwater/whatcauses.htm, last updated February 2002.

Notes:

1. Your teacher may want you to only list the texts you actually referred to in your essay. This is sometimes called a **reference list** instead of a bibliography.
2. There are other ways to set out your references (eg. date at the end of the reference, underline instead of italicise) so check if your teacher prefers a particular way. In general, however, being consistent with one method is the main thing.
3. If you can't find a date for a publication or website, write n.d (no date).
4. If you don't have an author or other originator of the text, use the name of the text for alphabetical ordering.
5. If you have more than one entry for one author, put them in order of the date of publication.

1 Look at this student's notes on the books, newspaper and website he has used.
Write out a bibliography using the information and examples above as your guide. Put your list in alphabetical order and number the entries from 1 to 6.

- *The Western News "Phone danger" p 17. Feb 16, 02 – Jackie Roach*
- *www.cleanup.com.au – Clean Up Australia Online – last updated 6th March 2002*
- *Science Today - June 2001 – "Are we safe?" Jill King – page 22 - 24*
- *Are our homes endangering our lives? J. Logan and L Todd, 2002, Blackman Publishing, Brisbane.*
- *'Looking into the future' video – Century 21 films. 2002*
- *J Logan and L Todd – Your local environment – 2000. Hill End publications. Melbourne*

In-text referencing

- As well as making a list of the texts you have used at the end of your essay, you must reference them *where you use them* in the essay itself. You have to do this both when you quote the exact words and when you use your own words.
- You don't have to put *all* the details in. Instead, you put just enough detail to show the reader where the information came from.
- This is usually the author's name, the year of publication and a page number (if text is more than one page). If the reader wants full information about the text, they can go to your bibliography.
- For example, if you wanted to include the idea from the text below:

  The greatest obstacle to acceptance of any e-book is the "Can I take it to bed with me?" syndrome ... If an e-book doesn't have an acceptable cuddle factor, most people who read for pleasure will remain bound to the analog version.
  (taken from Butler, M. "You got the book", Feature IT magazine, *The Weekend Australian*, Nov 14-15 1998, p. 11)

  You might write:
  As Butler (1998) has pointed out, the main obstacle to the acceptance of electronic books is the "Can I take it to bed with me?" syndrome.
  or
  One of the main obstacles to the acceptance of e-books is the feeling that they can't be read in bed (Butler, 1998).
  (No page number is needed here, because the article is only one page – your reader can get the full page reference from the bibliography.)

- Here are some other examples for other situations and types of texts:
  - for a book with two or three authors, you write all names, eg.
    A recent study (Milson & Kelly, 2001)
  - for a book with more than three authors, you write the first name plus *et al*, eg.
    (Zappa *et al*, 2000, p. 5)
  - for a text from an organisation, you write the name of the organisation, eg.
    25% of Australians now live alone (Australian Bureau of Statistics, 2001)
  - for a website, you give the name of the author or organisation if known, and the date the website was written or last updated, eg. (Environmental Protection Authority, online, 2001)
- There are a few different ways to do in-text referencing, and your teacher might want you to do it in a particular way, so make sure you check.

2 **a** Look at the sample essays in the Extras section and examine the way the in-text and bibliography references are done.

b Look also at the text in Task 4, Step 3, Section 4: *Including other people's ideas* (page 57), and examine the in-text reference examples there.

3 Read the two paragraphs below and then write sentences which refer to them. Use the patterns:
As Brown (1989, p. 65) has pointed out, ...
Jackson (2001, p. 90) mentions ...
Black (online, 2002, p. 4) raises one problem ...

a The overall influence of e-books on the environment remains unclear. Many of the earlier attempts at designing paperless systems not only failed, but may have ultimately produced more paper than necessary. The printing of electronic books may likewise actually use more paper than the printing press system of publication. For example, what good is an electronic copy of a document ... if everyone just prints it out, as opposed to using paper from a single copy and then circulating the document?
(taken from Xia Lin & Hubbard, J. *Books of the future*, online, http://www.pages.drexel.edu/~jmh29/653/final.pdf May 31 2000)

____

____

____

____

b People who have grown up with mobile phones tend to use their thumbs when others use their fingers. Today's twenty-somethings have become so adept at tapping out text messages on their mobiles that they now use their thumbs instead of their fingers for tasks such as ringing doorbells, pushing buttons and pointing. Sadie Plant, who founded the Cyberbetic Culture Research Unit at Warwick University, discovered this new behaviour when studying the effect of mobile phones on people's behaviour.
(taken from Murphy, M. 2001, "Fingers and thumbs", *New Scientist*, 3 November, Reed Publications, London, page 18)

____

____

____

____

WORK ON YOUR KEY ESSAY QUESTION

Look now at your essay draft.

Check to see if you need to add any in-text references or to fix up any errors.

Compile your bibliography following the examples in this section.

4 Using good spelling strategies

Most people worry about spelling when they are writing something important. Although a few spelling errors may not matter too much in some kinds of writing (eg. Internet chat or an e-mail to a close friend), they do matter in essay writing.

Why important?

Spelling mistakes work against the good ideas in your essay, distracting your reader from what you are saying. They also give a bad impression because they say loud and clear that you have not made the effort to find out the correct spelling.

What can you do? Spelling comes more naturally to some people than others, but everyone can improve their spelling with a few sensible strategies. Even the best spellers have a few words that always stump them and lead them to writing out a word a few different ways or checking the dictionary.

Spelling involves both sound and sight. Sure, sound is important but we can also *see* if a spelling is right or wrong. We remember the way a word *looks*. So working on remembering the visual image of a word is useful.

Look closely at your spelling when revising. Don't worry so much about it when drafting your essay, although it is a good idea to mark words you're unsure of.

If you really want to be a better speller, you have to develop your own sense of whether your spellings are right or wrong. Computer spell-checks or dictionaries and other people are all useful resources, but if you depend on them all the time you won't get much better. This student explains one of the problems with computer spell checks:

> *I always use the computer spell-check after I have finished typing my essay. It's great but sometimes I don't know which spelling to choose from those that they offer, and also, lots of my mistakes are correct spellings of other words. For example, I often write 'their' for 'there' and 'fell' for 'feel'. The computer doesn't pick these up.*

In this section we will look at some useful strategies to:

- identify spelling errors in your own writing
- spell unfamiliar words when you need them, and
- remember the spelling of words you find difficult.

HOT TIP!

Keep a list of your problem words and update it regularly. Put the list where you can see it often, for example, next to the bathroom mirror. Set yourself targets to learn certain words by a set date. Cross off the words when you are sure you know them.

Recognising your errors

Knowing you have spelt a word wrongly is the first step towards improving your spelling. If you are not sure about a word you have written:

- Ask yourself "Does it look right?"
- Say the word to yourself and ask "Have I got one or more letters for every sound I can hear?"
- Look through your essay draft – perhaps you spelt it correctly somewhere else.
- When writing your first draft, underline any words you think are wrong and keep going. Come back to check them later.

1 Look at this list of common words. Ten of them are spelt incorrectly. Underline the ones you think are wrongly spelt.

doesn't	wich	concentrate
companies	prefer	you'r
dicides	because	through
suitable	poeple	laugh
reveiw	sinse	devide
actualy	discussion	durring
straight	against	allmost

2 The incorrectly spelt words below should have at least one letter for each sound, but they do not. Can you add a letter or letters to make them correct?

nationalty	____________	indepedence	____________
personly	____________	delibrately	____________
considerble	____________	audence	____________
intrested	____________	critism	____________
basicly	____________	activties	____________
frighted	____________	cuture	____________

Spelling unfamiliar words and correcting errors

Some useful strategies for trying new words or correcting mistakes are:

- Write the word quickly. The correct spelling may come to your mind automatically.
- Write it a few different ways to see which way looks right.
- Write the letters you are sure about and leave a blank for the part you don't know. Try different ways to fill the blank.
- Think of other words that sound the same and try that spelling pattern.
- Use spellings of related words.
- Break the word into chunks.
- Make sure you have at least one letter for each sound you can hear.
- Use any spelling rules you know.
- Use the dictionary only after you have tried these strategies.

3 Look back at the wrongly spelt words in Task 1 above. Correct them now using some of the strategies above. Check your corrections using your dictionary.

4 Complete these words using the clues given.

a	med__ine	(clue: medical, medication)
b	si__n	(clue: signature, signal)
c	benef__t	(clue: beneficial)
d	separ__tely	(clue: separate)
e	mixt______	(clue: picture)
f	ra__ism	(clue: race)
g	__itizen	(clue: city)
h	gover__ment	(clue: govern)

5 Spelling rules can be tricky. One common spelling rule is about *ie* and *ei* but most people only know the first part:

'i' before 'e' except after 'c'. Here is the full rule:

'i' before 'e' except after 'c' and except where the sound is 'ay'. (There are some exceptions. The most important are: *their*, *either* and *neither*.)

These words all have either *ie* or *ei* missing. Use the rule to complete them.

a	bel______ve	**b**	rec______ve	**c**	th______f
d	rec______pt	**e**	pr______st	**f**	v______n
g	f______rce	**h**	n______ghbour	**i**	ach______ve
j	r______gn	**k**	v______l	**l**	f______ld

Remembering spellings

- When you are trying to remember a spelling, try to remember the way the word **looks**. Don't just copy a word lots of times or spell it out loud, although these methods are useful too.
- Use tricks to remember troublesome words eg. you might remember the *ie* part of *friend* because you have most time for seeing friends on FRIday or the weekEND.
- Use the following **Look - cover - write - check** method to actively memorise spellings:
  - Look at the word and really study it – first as a whole and then focusing on any difficult parts.
  - Cover the word and try to see it in your mind.
  - Write the word without looking back at it.
  - Check it. If it is right, write it one more time. If it is wrong, try again. Do this as often as you need to.
- Test your memory constantly afterwards. Write the word later in the day, the next day, after a week and so on.

6 Look over the last few pieces of writing you have done at school. Try the methods above on any words that you got wrong. Write the words on a list and put them somewhere where you will see them and learn them.

WORK ON YOUR KEY ESSAY QUESTION

Look through your essay draft very carefully. Have you misspelt any words? Correct them using the strategies above, and use the dictionary as a final check.

5 Getting the punctuation right

Read this:

> many students think that punctuation is a cruel invention which has no purpose at all except to make them lose marks and fail tests the truth however is that punctuation serves a very real purpose it helps us express exactly what we mean and it helps our readers understand that meaning this is particularly important in long and formal pieces of writing such as essays where our meanings are often very complex and where it is crucial for our reader to keep track of these complex meanings it is true that some punctuation is simply convention that is we do it a certain way because that is the way it has been done for a long time however we only follow these conventions because they work well to convey a meaning if they did not work well they would be thrown out by the people who use the language in other words by us.

OK how did you go? No doubt you eventually worked out what the words were all about. But you probably hesitated at least a few times to work out just how some words connected to others, and then had to re-read parts to make sure you had the whole meaning right.

Let's look at the same text now with punctuation (and some paragraphing).

> Many students think that punctuation is a cruel invention, which has no purpose at all except to make them lose marks and fail tests. The truth, however, is that punctuation serves a very real purpose. It helps us express exactly what we mean, and it helps our readers understand that meaning.
>
> This is particularly important in long and formal pieces of writing such as essays, where our meanings are often very complex, and where it is crucial for our reader to keep track of these complex meanings.
>
> It is true that some punctuation is simply convention. That is, we do it a certain way, because that is the way it has been done for a long time. However, we only follow these conventions because they work well to convey a meaning. If they did not work well, they would be thrown out by the people who use the language – in other words, by us.

Easier? I'm sure it was. In summary, punctuation is a very real part of the language. It helps us to make meaning and helps our readers understand that meaning.

Let's move on then to look at three aspects of punctuation that students often find difficult in essay writing.

HOT TIP!

The best way to improve your punctuation is to take notice of how the professionals do it. So read, read and read some more. Set aside time to think about why the writers have used a certain form of punctuation.

Tasks

PAGE 105

Full stops at the end of sentences

- All students know that you need to end a sentence with a full stop. The difficulty for many students, however, is in knowing where one sentence does actually end, and where the next one starts.
- This difficulty is very important to sort out because the writer's problem becomes the reader's problem. If the writer doesn't know where one sentence stops and another one starts, then neither will the reader. And then, of course, they will not understand what they are reading.
- In the section on *Writing grammatical sentences* you learnt what a sentence is. Here is that definition again:

  A sentence is a group of words that express a complete thought. This one definition is really the best test.
- If a group of words expresses a complete thought, then it is a sentence and needs to be followed with a full stop.
- If a group of words does not express a complete thought, you need to look at the group of words before it and after it, to see if they can be joined up to make a full sentence.
- If a group of words expresses more than one complete thought, you need to look at how the ideas can be broken up into two sentences.

(Look back at Step 4, Section 1, *Writing grammatical sentences* if you need to.)

1 Decide where to put the full stops in these sentences from different History essays. (Come back and look at these sentences again after you read about commas.)

a Henry VIII was the second son of Henry VII and Elizabeth of York Henry was being educated for the church but when his elder brother died Henry became heir to the throne.

b Henry's reign began with much feasting and sport after his father's solid rule the energetic youthful and handsome King avoided governing in person he preferred to journey the countryside hunting and reviewing his subjects.

c The Celtic people were not a united people though they had a common culture they were divided into tribes across various parts of Britain and Europe common traditions and language linked them so too did a close similarity in laws.

d Though males generally dominated Celtic society women had considerable freedom for example they could own their own property and even lead battles.

e As everyone had to farm for food most Celts were farmers who could also be part-time warriors or noblemen artists and other learned people were very highly regarded and this demonstrates a highly civilised culture.

f Alexander the Great lived a hard and rough life fighting battles and conquering land everywhere he went he lived to be thirty three years of age had he lived longer he may have conquered the whole world.

Commas

Commas are very important in helping to make our meanings clear.
We use commas to:

- divide up items in a list

  The Internet, e-mail, and mobile phones are now common methods of communication.
- divide up a sentence into clauses

  Although graffiti has a bad name, it should be considered as a form of art.
- separate linking words or other phrases from the rest of the clause or sentence

The Simpsons *is about a dysfunctional family in Springfield, USA, but, at the same time, it is about every family, in every country in the world.*

The Simpsons *is a satire and, like all good satires, it holds up a mirror to our lives.*

2 Look again at your sentences in Task 1. Add commas to the sentences where needed.

3 Use commas where needed in these sentences (from a history essay on ancient Greece).

a Although its exact origins are lost in time Greek religion is thought to date from about the 2nd millenium BC.

b The Greeks expected religion to explain natural phenomena such as lightning thunder and storms at sea.

c The ancient Greeks believed that temples were a place for gods to visit not as it sometimes thought a place of worship.

d Our earliest surviving examples of Greek literature are *The Iliad* and *The Odyssey* which record men's interactions with various gods and goddesses.

e Greeks believed that gods often spoke through oracles such as the Oracle of Apollo at Delphi in order to help humans understand the wishes of the gods.

f Before about 600BC the statues whether made of wood or stone seem to have been relatively small.

Apostrophes of omission and possession

- We use apostrophes for two reasons only — to show where we've left letters out or to show ownership or possession.
- We use an apostrophe to show that we have left a letter or letters out (the **apostrophe of omission**) eg. haven't (*have not*) , can't (*cannot*), it's (*it is*).
- A common mistake with this type of apostrophe is to confuse *its* and *it's*.
  - *its* is a possessive pronoun like *his* and *her*, but (like *his* and *her*) *its* does not need an apostrophe, eg:

  The nation soon fell into chaos. Its leaders appeared powerless to stop it.
  - *it's* means *it is, eg*:

  The Simpsons *is a comedy. It's (it is) about a family of five people.* (*Note*: It is generally advisable to use full forms eg. *it is, have not, cannot* in essays because contracted forms are too conversational.)

  You only use IT'S if you can replace it with IT IS and the sentence still makes sense.
- We also use an apostrophe to show a relationship of 'ownership' between two nouns (**apostrophe of possession**) eg. *the community's wishes, the workers' rights, the children's beliefs, the men's attitude.*

  The only rule you need to remember is this: The apostrophe comes immediately after the person or thing that does the owning. In the above examples – *the community, the workers, the children, the men.*
- A common mistake with this apostrophe is using it to show a plural form (more than one) when there is no ownership relationship, for example:

  The two princes' were killed in the Tower of London.

  The two countries' were at war.

  These sentences are **incorrect**: neither the princes or the countries 'own' any other noun in these sentences.

  The two princes were killed in the Tower of London.

  The two countries were at war.

  These are **correct**. We only need to show that we are talking about more than one prince and more than one country so we use *princes* and *countries*.

  Only use an apostrophe at the end of a noun if the noun owns another noun in the sentence.

4 Complete these sentences with *its* or *it's*.

a Biodiversity means the diversity of species on our planet. ______ role is vital to our survival as a species.

b A campaign to reduce stormwater pollution has been going for many years. ______ best known by the slogan "The drain is just for rain".

c *The Simpsons* is a popular show. Children usually love ______ slapstick humour.

STEP 4

d However, it can be difficult for children to appreciate ______ subtle humour.

e E-mail usage has increased dramatically in recent years. ______ particularly useful in the workplace.

5 Decide whether an apostrophe of possession is needed in the underlined words. If so, add one where needed.

a Only fifty to sixty percent of natural <u>forests</u> remain in the world today.

b Evolution occurs as a result of natural selective <u>forces</u>.

c Our <u>planets</u> survival could be under threat.

d <u>Australias</u> population is increasing now, but is expected to level off in the next few decades.

e Growth is occurring in all <u>states</u>.

f <u>Scientists</u> concerns are being ignored.

g <u>Politicians</u> views vary on the need for a population policy.

h There are <u>arguments</u> both for and against a population policy.

WORK ON YOUR KEY ESSAY QUESTION

Read through your essay draft looking particularly for the punctation features discussed here.

STEP FIVE

Do a final check

Congratulations, you have made it to the last but very important step – doing a final check of your essay.

By now you will have checked most aspects of your Key Essay Question, but this section gives you one more chance to improve it.

There are no tasks in this step. There is simply a checklist. The checklist covers all the points we have looked at in this book.

Read through it now and check your essay on each point.

1 A checklist for revising and editing your essay

General

- Is your essay on the general topic stated in the essay question?
- Does it address the particular topic focus stated in the essay question?
- Does it address the essay task eg. argue, discuss, explain?
- Is your essay organised in an appropriate way for the essay task?
- Are all the ideas and information related to the essay question?
- Do you have facts or evidence to back-up your opinions?
- Is your essay convincing?
- Does your essay have an Introduction-Body-Conclusion structure?

Introduction

- Is there a lead-in sentence which gives your reader some background or context?
- Is there a thesis statement which directly tells your reader your response to the essay question?
- Is there a preview or essay map which shows your reader what you are going to say in the Body Paragraphs?
- Are there any details that should not be there?

Body Paragraphs

- Have you defined or clarified any terms needed?
- Have you divided the Body of your essay into paragraphs?
- Is there only one main idea in each paragraph?
- Is there a topic sentence in each paragraph which states this main idea?
- Have you developed the topic sentence and not just repeated the one idea?
- Have you developed it in an appropriate way for the essay's purpose?

Conclusion

- Have you summarised the content of the Body Paragraphs?
- Is there a clear statement or restatement on the essay question?
- Have you avoided introducing any new points?
- Have you included any unnecessary detail?
- Does your Conclusion match your Introduction, but using different words?
- Does your Conclusion round off the essay in some way?

Language

- Do you need to make it easier for your reader to follow your ideas eg. by using linking words such as *however* or *as a result* or by reordering the ideas in your paragraphs?
- Is your language right for a formal written text and not too much like a conversation?
- Have you got complete and proper sentences?
- Have you checked all your spellings?
- Have you checked your punctuation?

References

- Do you have a bibliography or reference list arranged in alphabetical order?
- Have you put all necessary references within your essay?
- Have you paraphrased and summarised other people's words and not plagiarised?
- Have you put quotation marks where needed for exact words or phrases taken from someone else's work?

Extras

This section contains

1 Model Essay: summary of structure and language features
2 Stimulus material for Key Essay Questions
3 Sample essays on the Key Essay Questions
4 Ideas for practice essays

1 Model Essay: summary of structure & language features

STRUCTURE		LANGUAGE FEATURES
Introduction - lead-in (to give background) - thesis statement (main idea of essay) - essay map (tells reader what points to follow)	**Graffiti should be seen as a form of art. Do you agree or disagree?** Almost every week there is an article or letter in the newspaper on the subject of graffiti. Usually, the writers are complaining about quick and careless scrawls done on public or private property. This form of graffiti should not be considered as art, but other more complex and skilful forms should be. More advanced forms of graffiti brighten up our suburbs. These forms take great artistic skill to design and carry out. If they were recognised as art, young artists would have better opportunities to develop their skills and this would benefit the community.	Complete sentences throughout
Body Paragraphs define and clarify the essay question (to make argument)	It is important, first of all, to distinguish between three different types of graffiti. First, there is the 'tag' which is the stylised writing of the graffiti artist's name. Then, there is the 'throw-up' which is bigger and more time-consuming than the tag, but generally just big bubble letters in two colours. Lastly, there is the 'piece' (short for 'masterpiece') which takes considerable skill and time to execute. (Tucker, online, p. 3) Unfortunately most of what we see in our streets are tags and throw-ups and really just vandalism. They are generally done quickly and carelessly by people who do not think of themselves as artists. Pieces, on the other hand, are usually done by people who do see their work as art and themselves as artists.	Topic sentences in each body paragraph Linking words Words (especially pronouns) to refer back to things already mentioned
Point 1	If good graffiti is seen as art and then encouraged, it has the potential to improve the look of our streets and our transport systems. Good graffiti pieces are colourful, vibrant, and attractive. In most cases, they are far more attractive than the walls they are painted on, which in the old parts of cities are often ugly, dull and uncared for. There are many examples of spectacular murals in the inner city. In fact, some have even become tourist attractions. There are also excellent examples of graffiti on passenger or freight trains. However, because graffiti is usually seen as vandalism, no matter what the works look like, they are usually painted over in dull colours (Tucker, online p. 5).	Repetition of key words (graffiti) or words with similar meaning (murals, pieces) Reference to sources Word order helps reader to follow ideas
Point 2	Real graffiti pieces require high level artistic skill to design and carry out. Pieces are usually designed to cover very large areas such as walls, and so have to be planned in detail on paper first. The designs are usually intricate and involve many colours. They are usually done with spray cans and large textas, but some artists use paint rollers as well. Many pieces are just as good as what you can see hanging in art galleries, but because they are on the street and mostly done by young people, they are not considered as art.	Passives to put focus on processes etc

Point 3

Recognising talented graffitists as artists would give them the opportunity to further develop their skills. Graffiti artists need spaces where they can develop their spray can skills without breaking the law. In some parts of the city, there are legal walls and spaces, but in others there are very few or none at all. Most of the best examples of graffiti art can be found on walls where the artists have been given permission to do their work by councils or other organisations. This means they have the time to polish their work to a high artistic standard. If this happened more, the whole community would benefit.

Noun groups and nominalisations to pack meanings and to put focus where needed

Impersonal writing - no mention of writer or individuals

Conclusion
- summarises points
- restates thesis statement (main essay idea)

To sum up, there is more than one kind of graffiti. The more basic forms are generally not art. However, the more complex examples of graffiti are a form of art requiring considerable artistic skill. If these forms of graffiti were recognised as art, they could make our streets more attractive and, at the same time, give talented young artists an opportunity to develop their skills further and contribute their creative skills to their community.

Word to signal conclusion ie. to sum up

Bibliography:

Chalfont, H. & Prigoff, J. (1987) *Spraycan Art*. Thames and Hudson, London.

Tucker, D.O., (no date) *Graffiti: Art and Crime* (online) http://www-atdp-berkeley.edu/Studentpages/cflores/historygraffiti.html

Bibliography

2 Stimulus material for Key Essay Questions

Explain how mobile phones affect our lives.

1 "Almost everyone who wants a mobile phone – about 11 millon Australians – has one. Most of those who don't are probably under the age of 12, or can't afford one."
Lowe, S. (2001) "Brave New World" in *Sydney Morning Herald*, Dec 12, 2001, p. 11.

2 "We're witnessing the beginning of a wireless age in which everyone will be connected with everyone else, 24 hours a day, seven days a week."
Lindstrom, Martin (2002) "Message madness our big chance" in Next (IT supplement) of *Sydney Morning Herald*, Feb 26, p. 6.

3 "The charm of the mobile is that one can control who gets access to your number. I hardly ever give my number out, for example ... If I get a call it will be from my family or from work ...
Probably about half the mobile phones in circulation are not really on the public networks at all. They have become tiny networks, used only to link family members, or a group of schoolgirls or whatever.
What may be happening, indeed, is that we are giving people tools with which they can withdraw more closely into a small circle of people, mostly family, and regard the rest of the world with hostility..."
Waterford, Jack (2002) "Upwardly mobile on easy street", Panorama section of *The Canberra Times*, Jan 12, p. 20.

4 "Since a mobile phone is a sort of global positioning satellite system, constantly sending its location to the heavens, police and security agencies have discovered that it is a good way to follow criminals ..."
Waterford, Jack (2002) "Upwardly mobile on easy street", Panorama section of *The Canberra Times*, Jan 12, p. 20.

5 "Having trouble understanding what's being said on a newsgroup, mailing list or mobile phone near you? You're not alone ... what these people have in mind is the total destruction of the English language, and ultimately, Civilisation As We Know it.
It's worse on mobile phones, where an alternative language is being forced upon us which eliminates entire words, grammar and imaginative thought.
An extraordinary number of people no longer communicate by voice or writing. Increasingly what they are doing is 'texting' – sending shorthand communiques by mobile phone SMS message services.
This is being driven, of course, by the fact that it's a tedious affair to create with only 10 buttons the messages we are used to writing with 26 letters, plus punctuation."
Wright, Charles (2001) "O grammar where art thou?", E)MAG (magazine supplement), in *Sydney Morning Herald*, March, p. 28.

6 "Mobile phones are changing everything, everywhere ... school, families, fashion, friendships, churches, crime, courts, language: it's everybody's lifestyle now, whether you've got one or not.
Sure, manners may be lagging behind ... but with 65 per cent of Australians packing a portable, those phoning only from a fixed line can rage all they like about the rude intrusiveness of mobiles.
Even the penitent Franciscan friars have a phone habit now. The monks who dedicate themselves to missionary and humanitarian work, engaged a Milan designer to create new robes for them. According to *The Times*, they've updated to a snappy charcoal grey number ... with breast pockets for their mobile phones.
Michael Stevenson, a Monash University anthropologist, says mobile phones ... are great socialisers. 'They are not making us geeks with toys, isolated with our screens and text – they are creating tribes and connections.'
Martin, Lauren (2001) "Love in the time of mobiles" *Sydney Morning Herald*, Dec 12, p. 11.

7

Cartoon by Phil Somerville "The sum of us", Sunday Life (magazine supplement), *The Sun Herald*, Feb 24, 2002, p. 32.

The Simpsons does more than make us laugh. Do you agree or disagree?

1 "Tony Blair leads a country – Homer Simpson leads a life devoted to doughnuts. Tony Blair hob-nobs with heads of state – Homer hangs out in a dive bar.

So (now that Mr Blair is a father again) who should he look to as a role model? Yes, Homer Simpson.

At least, that's according to Lancaster University psychology professor Charlie Lewis who reckons that cartoon character Homer is one of the best examples of modern fatherhood.

He says many fathers could learn from Homer's fondness for watching TV with his children, to whom he's utterly devoted.

He said: '... the main place where fathers interact with their children is in front of the telly – much like Homer Simpson. Homer is a very good cultural icon for fathers.'

Apart from Bart, Homer is father to girls Maggie and Lisa and spends much of his time chauffering them about.

Homer does of course have a fondness for beer and food at his favourite haunt, the Frying Dutchman ... He also forgets birthdays and eats with his mouth open.

But Prof. Lewis pointed out: 'He has recently started going to parenting classes, so at least Homer is trying to be a good parent in his old age.'

"Top Dad Homer 'icon for Blair'", BBC News (online) Nov 19, 1999. http://news.bbc.co.uk/hi/english/uk/newsid 527000/527736.stm

2 "In a recent issue of ... a prestigious academic journal, Paul A. Cantor of the University of Virginia (wrote)

'For all its slapstick nature and its mocking of certain aspects of family life, *The Simpsons* has an affirmative side and ends up celebrating the nuclear family as an institution. For television, this is no minor achievement ...

In effect, the shows says 'Take the worst-case scenario – *The Simpsons* – and even that family is better than no family.'

Many people have criticized *The Simpsons* for its portrayal of the father as dumb, uneducated, weak in character and morally unprincipled. Homer is all those things, but at least he is there.'

Homer's virtue is seen in his staunch loyalty to his wife and children, Cantor writes. He points to an episode where Lisa ... yearns for a pony. To pay for it, Homer takes a second job working ... at the Kwik-E-Mart, almost killing himself in the process."

Lamey, Andy, "Simpsons revealed as models of family values", *National Post*, March 25, 2000, in *The Simpsons Archive*, http://www.snpp.com/other/articles/simpsonsrevealed.html last updated August 7, 2000 by Jouni Paakkinen.

3 "*The Simpsons* could help provide 'moral orientation' for those pondering the meaning of life, according to a Scottish academic.

Dr Kris Jozajtis, from Stirling University, said the cult television cartoon offered an ideal reference points to help religious teachers discuss morality ...

The show has been condemned by some fundamentalist church groups in the United States.

However, Dr Jozajtis said: '*The Simpsons* are in many ways a source of moral orientation, even on the big issues such as the meaning of life and where we came from. They seem to be anxious about these sort of questions and they worry about what is a good and moral way to live.

The Simpsons appeals to a wide variety of people and provides them with a very realistic view of how families deal with morally complex issues.' "

"Simpsons offer 'moral orientation'" BBC News (online) Feb 3, 2002-03-07 http://news.bbc.co.uk/hi/english/uk/scotland/newsid 1799000/1799183.stm

Books as we know them will disappear in the 21st century. Discuss.

1 "After more than 200 years, the Encyclopaedia Britannica has stopped printing books because its CD-ROM version is a far bigger seller.

It sells only a minimal number of books, compared with 150,000 CD-ROMs every year in Europe alone.

A full set of the bound volumes costs about $1,400 while the computerised version, containing the same information, is $199.

The British managing director, Mr James Strachan, said 'The economics of the encyclopaedia business mean it is far more profitable for us to concentrate on electronic publishing rather than book publishing.'

He said far more people bought the computerised version than ever bought the books, and consumers also find it more user-friendly."

"Britannic unbound as books abandoned", *Sydney Morning Herald*, July 29, 1999. p. 3.

2 "Whether you are a student, an office worker or a professional, sooner or later, you are going to need to use a dictionary.

Most of us baulk at stopping work to look up a word in that old dictionary we've more than likely carried with us since the start of high school ... The solution is to have the dictionary on your computer, a click away ... A proper electronic dictionary allows you, mid-sentence, to check spellings, find meanings and synonyms of words, and gives examples of word use in sentences ...

The latest trend is to have the dictionary permanently online via a Web site."

Archee, Ray (2002) "The last word", Icon, *Sydney Morning Herald* Feb 23-24, p. 16.

3 "Books have souls. Or so romantics like me tend to think. However pro-technology and pro-future I get, I still have a deep love for printed and bound texts ... neither the Internet nor computers really threaten the book as an art form."

Rushkoff, Douglas (1997) "People, not computers, kill books" Syte, in *The Weekend Australian*, 24-25 May, p. 3.

4 "Book lovers will wax lyrical about the smell of a new book, the feel of the cover, the whisper of the pages as they are turned. And then there's the joy of adding a book to the collection on the shelves and creating a personal literary timeline.

They're portable too. You can take books to the beach, read them in the bath, and, though battered and wrinkled, they will still be usable.

But as we stand on the edge of the third millenium, the humble book is being joined (or usurped, depending on your point of view) by the e-book, in a shift not seen since Johannes Gutenberg began printing Bibles in the 15th century ...

The book of the future, says the Ist Books site (an online library) 'is available 24 hours a day, 365 days a year, to anyone on the planet with a connection to the Internet, at a fraction of the cost of a conventional book. There is no paper or ink, binding, wrappng, postage, or costs for transporting truckloads of heavy boxes from place to place ... Not a single tree is felled in the manufacturing process. Not one sheet of paper enters the waste stream, clogs a landfill or pollutes the air after burning in a waste incinerator."

Austin, Keith (1991) "Sign of the tomes" Icon, *Sydney Morning Herald*, May 29, p. 4.

5 "... so far, books are the one information consumable that have resisted replacement by digital technology. Music has moved from vinyl records to cassettes ... CDs, DAT tapes and now MP3. The moving image has migrated from file to videotape to DVD, and the still (image) from film to silicon. Both now stream from the desktop as multimedia.

Books are proving more stubborn. It is nearly two years since the first e-books were launched in the US, but there and in Europe they have won less than one per cent of the book-buying market."

Knox, Malcolm (2000) "The book is dead, long live the book" E)MAG (magazine supplement) *Sydney Morning Herald*, June p. 18.

6 "E-book manufacturers are betting that changing consumer attitudes, driven by the explosion of Internet use in recent years and the ready acceptance of hand-held devices ... have created a new and sympathetic market.

The greatest obstacle to acceptance of any e-book is the "Can I take it bed with me?" syndrome. Books – even the tackiest, well-read paperback – are intimate, tactile objects as well as portable repositories for words, images and ideas, and if an e-book doesn't have an acceptable cuddle factor, most people who read for pleasure will remain bound to the analog version."

Butler, Mark (1998) "You got the book", Feature IT magazine, *The Weekend Australian*, Nov 14-15, p. 11.

3 Sample essays on the Key Essay Questions

Explain how mobile phones affect our lives.

Approximately 11 million Australians or 55% of the population own mobile phones. Most of those who don't are probably young children or people who can't afford one (Lowe, 2001). It is clear then that mobile phones are affecting our lives in many ways. The positive effects include convenience in everyday life and usefulness in emergencies. The negative effects include a decrease in privacy, and the intrusion they make on other people's lives in public spaces.

One of the great benefits mobile phones bring is day-to-day convenience. For example, mobiles are used by millions of people every day to arrange transport. Parents often use them to arrange pick-ups of children from railway stations, or from sports or social events. In fact, many parents buy their children mobile phones just for this purpose. They would rather spend the money on phones, than have their children waiting around deserted streets because of problems with arrangements. Mobile phones are also used a great deal between teenage friends when out. Instead of making an arrangement to meet at a certain time, they leave their arrangements until they are in the area and then communicate by phone to say exactly where they are. These everyday uses of mobile phones look likely to expand much further. In Japan, there are mobiles on the market with digital cameras built in, that allow you to take a photo, and then send it as an e-mail attachment to a friend anywhere in the world.

Mobile phones are also very useful in emergency situations. For example, if a road accident or a breakdown happens, we can use a mobile to report it to the emergency road services or to the police. Waving someone down to ask them to ring at the next town is now a thing of the past. If on a bushwalk nowadays, a mobile phone is seen as an essential piece of equipment for reporting accidents or summoning help if lost. The difference that mobile phones make in our lives in emergencies was shown dramatically in the September 11th tragedy, when World Trade Centre workers and passengers on the doomed flights were able to phone their families, to let them know what was happening and to say their last goodbyes.

However, not all effects of mobile phones on our lives are positive. Privacy is non-existent if you own a mobile. People you may not want to talk to can find you wherever you are. People can contact you any time and any place and getting away from people can be nearly impossible. This is especially a problem for people who work. If they have a mobile, their boss can call them at any time and expect them to answer the phone. Even if you turn off your phone, people can leave a message and ask you to ring back. As technology advances, it may be even harder to have any private time. Some people think that we are at "the beginnings of a wireless age in which everyone will be connected with everyone else, 24 hours a day, seven days a week" (Lindstrom, 2002).

If you are not the one whose privacy is being intruded upon with a phone call, then someone around you will be. First, there is the annoying ring of the phone interrupting the silence. Then there is the conversation. People speak on phones on public transport every minute of the day, and it can be very irritating to hear a loud half-hour conversation going on in the next seat when you are trying to read a book or have a rest. People seem to speak more loudly than normal on mobile phones so it is usually hard to ignore these conversations. When people are told to turn off their mobiles in theatres and cinemas, most do but some people decide that their conversations are more important than the comfort of others and keep them on. With more and more people using mobile phones, this sort of problem will only get worse.

Mobile phones make our lives easier in everyday situations and in emergencies, but there are drawbacks to their use too, especially in the way they interfere with privacy. Whether we like them or not, however, it looks like mobile phones are here to stay and that more and more people will use them. Most will take advantage of the benefits they bring and either ignore or find a way around the drawbacks.

Reference list:

Lindstrom, M. (2002) "Message madness our big chance", NEXT (IT supplement), *Sydney Morning Herald*, Feb 26, p. 6.

Lowe, S. (2001) "Brave New World", *Sydney Morning Herald*, Dec 12, 2001, p. 11.

by Hamish McLean

The Simpsons does more than make us laugh. Do you agree or disagree?

The Simpsons is a television cartoon show that has been running for many years. It contains five main characters, all members of the Simpson family. There is Homer, the slow-witted father, Marge, the conscientious mother and wife, Bart, the mischievous young boy, Lisa, the intellectual younger sister and Maggie, the overlooked baby of the household. Every episode of *The Simpsons* teaches us a moral lesson, proving that it does more than make us laugh. Three examples will demonstrate this.

Many episodes focus on the importance of family. One example is the episode where the family dog, Santa's Little Helper, gets sick and requires an operation to save him. This operation costs a lot and the Simpsons can hardly pay for it. Some big sacrifices have to be made by them all. They decide together that they would much rather part with money than part with a family member. There are numerous other episodes like this one, where we see that, although the Simpsons make a lot of mistakes, they do love and care about each other. These sorts of episodes are good examples of how *The Simpsons* does more than make us laugh.

Other episodes makes us think about what life is all about. One episode, for example, teaches the important lesson that you should value your life because it can be taken away as quickly as it is given. In this episode, Homer is thought to have swallowed a deadly part of a blowfish. The doctors give him twenty-four hours to live. In that time, Homer dreams that he does all the things he has ever really wanted to do but has not accomplished in his lifetime so far. Homer wakes to find he has not died and that the doctors had been wrong in their diagnosis. The episode reminds us that *The Simpsons* is not only a comedy.

Many episodes contain lessons about how we should behave towards others. In one episode, where Mr Burns is shot, the lesson is not to jump to believe the worst about people whenever we hear it. Mr Burns is a millionaire and is the boss of the nuclear plant where Homer works. When he is shot, everyone in town is suspected of the murder. When Mr Burns wakes in a daze but is still not thinking clearly, he believes that Homer has shot him. Homer is arrested but escapes, and is then hunted down. Only his daughter, Lisa, believes that he is innocent. After Mr Burns recovers properly, he explains that Homer has been wrongfully accused. Again, the show demonstrates that there is much more to it than comedy and laughter.

These episodes are only three of many hundreds. It would be possible to examine each one of these for a deeper, more serious level of meaning. During every half hour screening of *The Simpsons* there is something for both adults and children to think about and learn from. The show does far more than make us laugh. Perhaps this is why it has run for so long and has a cult following among young and old.

by Sam Tompkins

Books as we know them will disappear in the 21st century. Discuss.

Over the ages, books have developed and changed, from the times of the inkpot and quills, when all books were handwritten in Latin, to these days when thousands of books are printed at a time. At this point at the beginning of the 21st century, we have come to expect that books will be there for us to read and enjoy forever. But times change, trends differ and technology advances. It is now fair to say that we are in the computer age. As we move further forwards with technology, will we be leaving our books behind us?

These days we are definitely drifting further towards the Internet for all our research needs. As the Internet is a quite fast and efficient service, it is seen as the smarter way to find what we are looking for. There is information on nearly every possible topic imaginable and from many and varied sources. The Internet enables us to gain information, just as we would from a book or encyclopaedia, but minus the trouble of going to the library, finding the book and then looking inside it for the information. As technology advances and the Internet becomes more and more efficient, it is gaining a reputation for being the first and sometimes the only source to go to when we need to research a subject.

However, all things have disadvantages. Just as books may be seen as difficult to locate and then find the information in, the Internet can be more of a hindrance than a help on occasions. As the Internet has a large base of information, locating exactly what we need is sometimes quite a trying task. In some instances we find that it probably would have been easier to have gone to the library and used a book. Another problem we are faced with while searching on the Internet is whether or not the information is correct. We sometimes can be deceived by information on a website and be unaware that what we are writing down is incorrect.

Books have been with us for many thousands of years, and are commonly used for enjoyment purposes. Reading stories in books is an ancient pastime, and although the variety of activities we can undertake in our spare time has increased dramatically over the years, it is still quite common to read books. Many people would probably say that they find reading a book more relaxing and better for the mind than watching television or looking at a computer screen. Books, of course, are not only used for enjoyment purposes. They are used for education too, and play a major part in primary and secondary schooling and in tertiary study.

One disadvantage, however, of using books is that they are most commonly made from paper, and of course, paper comes from trees – trees which have had to be cut down. Thus the manufacture of books contributes to deforestation. From an environmental point of view, using sources other than paper books for reading purposes would do less damage to our forests. Trees would be able to regenerate and this would contribute generally to a better world environment.

As the computer age takes over, we may use books less, especially for information purposes. However, books as we know them will not disappear completely in the 21st century, as they are too important to our daily lives. We take books for granted, but take them away and we would quickly understand how often they are called upon. Even if the Internet becomes more efficient, reliable and authoritative, for enjoyment purposes it will never replace the book. Books link us to our origins, our traditions, our history and our future. Books are too special to us all to disappear.

Bibliography

1. Archee, Ray (2002) "The last word", Icon, *Sydney Morning Herald*, Feb 23-24, p. 16.
2. Austin, Keith (1991) "Sign of the tomes", Icon, *Sydney Morning Herald*, May 29, p. 4.
3. "Britannic unbound as books abandoned", *Sydney Morning Herald*, July 29, 1999. p. 3.
4. Butler, Mark (1998) "You got the book", Feature IT magazine, *The Weekend Australian*, Nov 14-15, p. 11.
5. Knox, Malcolm (2000) "The book is dead long live the book", E)MAG (magazine supplement) *Sydney Morning Herald*, June p. 18.
6. Rushkoff, Douglas (1997) "People, not computers, kill books", Syte, in *The Weekend Australian*, 24-25 May, p. 3.

by Hana Marjanac

4 Ideas for practice essays

Here is a list of essay questions that you could use for extra practice. All are general interest topics that you probably already know something about from everyday school and community life.

1 Violent video and computer games should be banned. Do you agree or disagree?
2 Space exploration is a waste of time. Do you agree or disagree?
3 There is absolutely no point in school uniforms. Discuss.
4 Explain some of the ways in which advertisements influence adolescents.
5 What do you predict will be the major achievements of the 21st century?
6 Cloning will only bring disaster for mankind. Discuss.
7 Why is reality TV so popular?
8 Would it have been better to grow up in your parents' day? Compare and contrast lives now and then to support your view.
9 How could we encourage people to use their cars less?
10 The search for aliens is a waste of time. What do you think?
11 Choose an invention of the 20th century and describe its influence on our lives.
12 Australia's interest in sport is unhealthy. Discuss the arguments on both sides of this statement.
13 Trace the development of popular music over any period during the last 50 years.
14 Zoos should be closed down. Do you agree?
15 Do you believe that Australia is successful as a multicultural nation?
16 The media is the most important influence on adolescent behaviour. Do you agree?
17 Choose a character in a book and list the similarities and differences between that character and yourself.
18 What are some of the ways we could stop people littering?
19 We should all throw away our TV sets. Discuss.
20 Progress always benefits mankind. To what extent do you think this is true?

Answers

STEP ONE

UNDERSTAND ABOUT ESSAYS

1 What exactly is an essay? page 4

1 The essay writer partly agrees and partly disagrees with the essay question.

The writer makes a statement about this view in the sentence: This form of graffiti should not be considered as art, but other more complex and skilful forms should be.

The writer makes three points to support this statement after first clarifying three different kinds of graffiti. The points are:

- If good graffiti were seen as art, it has the potential to improve the look of our streets and transport systems.
- Real graffiti pieces take artistic skill.
- Recognising talented graffitists as artists would let them develop their skills further.

The writer:

- tells you about what she is going to write about in the first paragraph (the Introduction)
- writes about it in paragraphs 2-5 (the Body Paragraphs)
- tells you what she has written about in the last paragraph (the Conclusion).

2 **a** Graffiti is simply a modern version of this ancient artistic tradition.

b Graffiti is nothing more than vandalism and should never be considered as a form of art.

c Graffiti is a new form of art and should be made legal.

d There is no way that this destructive activity should ever be considered as art.

3 **a** This paragraph does not clearly support or develop the statement on the essay question made in the first paragraph. The first sentence does not link the paragraph with the essay question at all, and the first two examples take the focus even further away from the topic. The paragraph could be made relevant if it was rewritten to link it clearly with the essay question.

b This paragraph is like part of an everyday conversation. It relates a personal experience which **is** relevant to the essay question, but it is not written in a way that is appropriate to an essay. The writer could use this personal experience but would need to write about it in a more formal, impersonal way.

2 Why do we write essays? page 8

1 **a** Opinion. 'Sadness' is a response to the story. One person might find it sad but another might not. If the person had said "I found the story very sad." it might be factual if for example he/she had cried.

b Factual. Can be proven by census information.

c Opinion. Writer could argue that this is so by quoting from the novel.

d Opinion. No way to prove that this is true.

e Opinion. Any statement about the future is opinion because it can't be proved. However there may be good evidence to support such an opinion.

f Factual. Can be proven by research.

g Factual. Can be proved by statistics.

h Factual. Can be proven by examination of objects used in religious ceremonies, written records and so on.

2 **a** F
b O
c O
d F
e F
f O
g O
h F

Matching opinions and facts: b and d; c and h; f and a; g and e.

3 **a** This essay is more about what the writer thinks (opinion). However, she also uses some facts to support her view eg. definitions of different types of graffiti, some graffiti becoming a tourist attraction, how graffiti is actually done. The mix of opinion and fact is appropriate to the essay question. There is no one right or wrong answer to this type of question. You have to argue for your opinion and use facts where you can.

b Personal response.

c Purpose is to argue for or against a case or point of view, that is, that graffiti should be seen as a form of art.

3 How is an essay different from everyday speech and other written texts? page 10

1 **a** paragraph 1 (Introduction)
b paragraph 5
c last paragraph (Conclusion)
d paragraph 3
e paragraph 2
f paragraph 4

Some of the differences are: many references to the speaker eg. *I don't think, I've thought about this*; casual conversational language eg. *I reckon, some guys, a fair bit*; talking directly to the listener/asking questions eg. *Let me tell you ..., Have you ever ...? You don't seriously think ...?*

2 Essay is extract *e*. The writer develops the idea that 'some technological progress has not been beneficial for society' using fact and opinion; writer focuses on general things eg. 'weapons' and groups of people eg. 'nations, families and individuals'. Seems like the writer is trying to convince the reader; the writing is formal

Other texts are:
a speech script
b story
c report
d book review.

Some of the features of these types of writing:

- Speech includes words referring to the speaker and what she did eg. 'I researched', 'I thought'; speaker talking about specific people and incidents; language shows she is talking directly to an audience eg. 'this article', 'listen to'.
- Story uses imaginative language eg. 'closing its grip'; incomplete sentences and repetition used for dramatic effect eg. 'The screams. The screams. The screams'; writer focuses on a specific person and her experience.

- Report is largely factual; descriptive and specialised musical terms eg. 'freewheeling, jazzy'; writer focuses on specific individuals.
- Book review identifies book and author and general theme, following typical pattern of first part of a review; writing about a specific book and characters.

4 Are all essays the same? page 12

1 **a** E
b A
c E
d A
e D

2 **i - b**
ii - d
iii - a
iv - c
v - e

3 **a** discusses both sides of an issue
b explains something
c argues a point of view

5 What is the basic essay structure? page 14

1 The Introduction of the Model Essay prepares the reader for the fact that there are different types of graffiti and the arguments the writer will make to support her position on the issue.

The Conclusion refers back to the distinction between different types of graffiti and to each of the arguments in the Body.

HELP! TASK

- There is a statement which briefly and directly tells the reader the student's response to the essay question but it is the very last sentence. The writer should tell us this in the first paragraph. In the first paragraph, the writer tells us that she hates graffiti but that does not really answer the question about graffiti as art.
- The essay is almost totally opinion apart from the experience of seeing someone doing graffiti. The writer needs more fact and more development of her opinions. It is really only in the last paragraph that the writer gets onto the essay question. The earlier paragraphs are off the question – talking about what should happen to people who do graffiti and what can be done about the problem.
- The essay is not very convincing because there is so little fact or development of opinion; because the writer is rather emotional about the subject eg. '... I hate it'; and because she does not really stick to the question.
- The essay does put forward arguments but they are on indirectly related topics eg. what should happen to graffiti artists. The essay does not present an argument for or against the statement in the essay question.
- The essay generally does not use the right kind of language for an essay. It is too conversational and too much about personal experiences and feelings, eg. 'The other day I was walking ...', 'When I told my mum ...', 'While I have been writing this essay I have been thinking ...', ' the really good stuff'.
- The essay looks like there might be an Introduction-Body-Conclusion structure, but there is not. The writer does not introduce what she is going to say, and then say it.

STEP TWO

PREPARE FOR WRITING

1 Understanding the essay question page 17

2 **a** Cloning will only bring disaster to mankind. Discuss*.
b How does* space exploration benefit the human race?
c What were some of the main differences* between the ancient Olympic Games and the modern Olympic Games? ('some of the main' narrows down the topic)
d Trace* the development of popular music over any 20-year time period of this century.
e Discrimination against youth is on the rise. Do you agree?
f What are the main causes* of global warming? ('the main' narrows down the topic)
g What events* led to the French Revolution?
h Who was* Alexander the Great and what were* his major achievements? (there are two topics in this essay question; 'major' narrows the focus of the second topic)

3 **b** The Introduction makes a statement which gives an opinion on the essay question.

4 **c** The Introduction makes a statement which sets up the discussion topic by asking a question.

5 **a - iii**
b - ii
c - xi
d - v
e - viii
f - vi
g - i
h - vii
i - xii
j - iv
k - xiii
l - xiv
m - ix
n - x

3 Doing the research page 26

1 The first paragraph suggests that it is going to be about the possibilities of electronic books. It says that it does not think it is going to be either books or technology, and says that printing is just an evolving (changing) technology.

4 **a** Standardised spelling, paragraphs and punctuation (just like hyperlinks).
b Any three of the following disadvantages: rapidly disintegrating spines, greasy feeling paper, squinty print, shoddy colour separation, subject to acid disintegration, easily damaged, quickly out of print, bulky to store, back-breaking to move, mouldy smelling and visually dull.
c His ideas are based on reports of the developing technologies.
d The electronic book would run on a watch battery which needs replacing only once every three years.
e It would be good for his eyes because the text's font could be changed to suit his ageing eyes. Also the screen would be softly glowing, back-lit and glare-free.
f You could switch to the text reader if you started falling asleep.

g You could write notes with a pen on the touch-sensitive screen or via the keyboard on electronic sticky notes.

5 a There are many ideas which support this idea eg. the book would be padded and soft (bound in calfskin). It does not weigh much; it is available in a variety of sizes; it has a softly glowing, back-lit, glare-free screen so you don't disturb others; you could switch to the text reader when you start to fall asleep.

b It can be downloaded from the local bookshop for a fraction of the cost of a paper version because you are not buying paper, which is expensive to make, bind into books, store, transport and shelve.

c We've all seen the potential that digitised information has had for education: computer-assisted instruction, multi-media books for beginner readers and of course the Internet.

6
- The author is Doug Johnson, who is the District Media Supervisor for the Mankato Public Schools, Mankato, Minnesota in the USA.
- He is an 'expert' of a kind because he works in education, and especially in media. His article has already been published in a technology magazine. (It says at the end of the article: Reprinted with permission from *Technology Connection: The Magazine for School Media and Technology Specialists*).
- You could therefore feel confident that his ideas were based on technology reports even though they are 'imaginings' of what might be possible (so only opinions).
- You could quote him to provide some evidence that these sorts of developments are possible. You could also use the text just to give you some ideas to get going.
- The text was written in 1998. In this case, you could assume that technology has moved on since then and we are much closer to seeing these developments. Generally however, an old date would make you think carefully about how up-to-date the ideas or information were. You might look for more recent information.

4 Organising your ideas page 31

2
- The writer of the graffiti essay has a view somewhere in between agreeing and disagreeing.
- Yes. Paragraph 2 clarifies and defines the essay question by distinguishing between types of graffiti.
- The writer does this because it is important to her overall view that some graffiti is not art but some graffiti is.
- There is no paragraph which gives a view which opposes the writer's own view.
- The writer gives three arguments to support her view:
  - if good graffiti were seen as art, it has the potential to improve the look of our streets and transport systems
  - real graffiti pieces take artistic skill
  - recognising talented graffitists as artists would let them develop their skills further.

5 Doing a detailed plan page 37

1 Sample answers for essay plan:
Paragraph 3 — argument 2 – real pieces take artistic skill to design and carry out:
- very large, on walls
- need to plan in detail
- intricate designs, colours
- methods
- some as good as paintings in art galleries

Paragraph 4 — argument 3 – recognising talented graffitists as artists would give them better chance to develop skills:
- need spaces where they are not breaking law
- some legal walls but not many
- best examples on legal walls because artists have time to do work well
- whole community would benefit if more legal walls

HELP! TASK

- The essay plan is on the general topic ie. books and generally on the topic focus ie. whether or not books will disappear in the 21st century.
- The essay plan does not address the essay task eg. to discuss. It does not put forward points on either side of the issue. Instead it focuses on one side ie. that books will not disappear.
- The plan is not organised appropriately for a discussion essay with arguments for and against. Also, instead of posing the essay question in the Introduction and then answering it in the Conclusion, the writer plans to give his view in the Introduction. If he followed this plan in the essay, the reader would not get the impression that the writer had carefully weighed up each side of the case.
- The history of printing seems off the topic and task.
- The plan is generally not very detailed, but it may be enough to guide this student.
- The plan is relatively easy to follow with numbered points suggesting what each paragraph will be about.

STEP THREE
MAKE A FIRST DRAFT

1 Drafting the Introduction page 43

2 a Street art has been around for a very long time. People were painting on cave walls thousands of years ago. Graffiti is simply a modern version of this ancient artistic tradition. * It is only because it is on the street and not in an art gallery that people are so negative towards it.

b Many of the streets in our cities have been destroyed in recent years by graffiti. Graffiti is nothing more than vandalism and should never be considered as a form of art. The costs to the individuals and to the community in general are enormous.

c Graffiti is a new form of art and should be seen as such. *However, this is unlikely to happen because of prejudice in our community against youth and their interests and activities.

d Graffiti has become a very big problem in our cities and towns. Huge amounts of public money are being spent cleaning it up. There is no way that this destructive activity should ever be considered as art. * It is generally very ugly and usually done simply to irritate the authorities and members of the public.

3 These sentences are too detailed for this Introduction:
I have read some letters which use words like 'scum' and 'brainless vandals'.
This money could be spent providing youth and other community services.

4 The correct order of the sentences of the Introductions are:
The Simpsons: b, d, a, c
Mobile phones: d, a, b, e, c (*Note*: e and c could be the other way around although it would be more usual to put the positive effects first)
Future of books: b, d, e, a, c

HELP! TASK

- This Introduction begins with the thesis statement (first sentence). This is OK but it might have been better to begin with a lead-in which says what *The Simpsons* is about.
- The thesis statement does relate back to the question but it does not clearly tell us what the writer is saying on the question. It is a little vague.
- There is no preview or essay map.
- Most readers would probably say they had very little idea of what the writer would say in the Body after reading this.
- The writer includes an unnecessary detail about one of the characters, Mr Burns.
- Most readers would probably say that the Introduction does not make them feel confident that the writer knows what he is talking about. This is because there is no specific information about what the essay will focus on, and because the statement of the writer's view is quite vague.
- The last sentence is also a problem. It does not really add anything useful to the Introduction.

2 Drafting the Body Paragraphs

page 47

2 Topic sentences are:

a Black Americans of the 1950s and 1960s had a difficult life.
b The thinning of the ozone layer is being caused by a family of gases discovered about 50 years ago called chlorofluorocarbons (CFCs).
c There are three types of volcanoes.
d "The Road Not Taken" is one of the best examples of Frost's gentle symbolism.
e The physical attributes needed for a sprinter are different from those required for a marathon runner.

3 **i** - **a**
ii - **e**
iii - **d**
iv - **b**
v - **c**

4 Sentences which do not relate are:

a They obviously had the ability to think and solve problems and work together.
b The nurse had some responsibility because she brought the two together.

5 The matching topic sentences are:

i c One source that tells us that the ancient Olympic Games were significant was the Olympic Truce.
ii a There is some doubt about the original purpose of the ancient Olympic Games.
iii b The procedures and practices of the ancient Olympic Games were different to the modern Olympic Games.

6 The four paragraphs begin with these sentences:
Knights were very important in medieval England.
The weapons for the knights stayed basically the same all through the Middle Ages.
Swords were very highly valued.
Knights also fought with a lance, a kind of long spear that could reach up to fifteen feet in length.

HELP! TASK

- The paragraph has more than one idea. It begins by talking about the portability of books, then moves to the feel of books, and other attractions. It then returns to the portability topic in the last sentence but shifts the focus to electronic books.
- The first sentence appears to be the topic sentence and is expressed quite clearly. However, as already said, the paragraph does not keep to the topic of the topic sentence.
- The writer begins to develop the topic sentence in an appropriate way, but then loses focus, and the writer ends by almost contradicting herself, that is, saying that perhaps there is not much difference between the portability of paper books and electronic books.
- The writer does not fully develop the paragraph in an appropriate way for a discussion essay.

3 Drafting the Conclusion page 51

2 a A-ii, B-iii, C-i

b i <u>While older people hold onto their stereotypical views of youth</u>, graffiti will never be seen as art. Youth and community workers should however be working to change these views. If they do, perhaps one day graffiti will take its place as a legitimate form of art.

ii <u>Graffiti is no different from the wall drawings and paintings that have been done from the beginning of man's time on Earth</u>. While not everyone may like it, it is a form of artistic expression and should not be illegal.

iii Graffiti is not art. <u>It is simply destruction of public and private property</u>. If the people who carry out this vandalism are made to clear it up, then we might not see so much of it in the future.

3 a Conclusion A – discuss; Conclusion B – explain
Conclusion C – compare /contrast; Conclusion D – argue

<u>Overall</u> the positive and negative effects of TV ...
<u>To conclude</u>, life at the turn of the last century was very different ...
<u>To sum up</u>, there is no good reason to wear school uniforms ...

4 These sentence-parts are too detailed for this Conclusion:
... such as human sacrifices, the displaying of decapitated heads and going to war naked.

... for example the equality of women, religious practices and astronomy, the skills in metal work and art and the immense respect for bards and Druids, and the fact that rulers could be elected.

HELP! TASK

- There is a restatement on the essay question ("*The Simpsons* does more than make us laugh") but as in the Introduction, the statement is rather vague and does not say in what way the show does more than make us laugh
- The writer follows this sentence with more information about it being funny which goes against the main statement of view.
- However, the writer does then make points about why the show does more than make us laugh. These points might refer to ideas in the essay Body or they might be new points – we can't be sure. The points do not seem to be a summary.
- The detail about Homer is unnecessary.
- The Conclusion matches the Introduction in its main idea – that the show does do more than make us laugh. It also refers again to how long the show has run.
- The last sentence rounds off the essay.
- The writer does use different words from the Introduction 'a great comedy' vs 'very, very funny', 'it is really more than that' vs 'does more than make us laugh'; 'longest running cartoon of all time' vs 'have run for so long.'

4 Including other people's ideas

page 55

2 Sample answers

a (Future of books)

Electronic books would have to have some kind of mechanism to turn pages to be really acceptable to most people, because this so much part of their book reading experience.

One thing people like about books is the way they turn the page to get to the next interesting bit, so electronic books would have to include something that was like this to be accepted by the general population.

b (Mobile phones)

There are some places that mobile phones simply are not acceptable to most people, so devices that could automatically turn off phones in these areas would probably be welcomed by the majority.

Although most people turn off their phones in places like movie theatres or aeroplanes, there is a need for external devices in these places that would automatically turn off mobiles. Most of the population would probably not object to such devices.

c (*The Simpsons*)

Both adults and children enjoy *The Simpsons* though perhaps not for the same reasons. Children respond more to the obvious jokes whereas adults understand the less obvious jokes and the underlying moral messages.

Adults probably watch *The Simpsons* in a different way to children but both seem to enjoy it very much. Adults probably tune in for the sophisticated humour and deeper meaning whereas children probably watch it just for the laughs.

5 Sample answer:

There is no clear evidence either way about the effect of TV viewing on children. Some research suggests that there are no negative effects and that children are quite discriminating about what they watch and how they watch. Some research suggests that they actually do not watch as much as is often thought, and that generally they watch suitable programs. However, other studies are more alarming and suggest that children watch far too much TV and that the effects are harmful for both children's minds and bodies.

5 Making your essay 'hang together'

page 59

3 **a** Nevertheless
b For this reason
c In the first place/For example
d Eventually
e Furthermore
f For example/In the first place

4 **a** *Homo habilis*
b Items they crafted
c More elaborate tools than those created by *Homo habilis*
d *Homo sapiens*
e Achievements such as setting stone into wooden bases to make spears and knives
f *Homo sapiens*
g Rock wall art
h The purpose of rock wall paintings
i The rituals which took place in large caves
j The purpose of rock wall paintings

5 **d, a, e, c, b**

6 **c, d, a, b, e**

HELP! TASK

- Repeat *paper books* in the second sentence and use instead of *they*.
- Reorder the words in the third sentence to keep the focus on *paper books*, but use *they* instead of books.
- Put a linking word at the beginning of the fourth sentence to show the contrasting idea, eg. *however, on the other hand, nevertheless.*
- Put a linking word at the beginning of the fifth sentence to show how it connects with the fourth sentence, eg. *in fact, actually*
- Link up the last two sentences with *and.*

These changes would give the following paragraph which is far more cohesive than the original:

It is difficult for many people to imagine a world where there will be more electronic books than paper books. Paper books will not disappear. They will be used alongside computer texts. However, there will be more and more information texts placed on computer. In fact, most encyclopaedias are already on computer, and many encyclopaedia companies no longer publish print versions.

STEP FOUR

REVISE AND POLISH

1 Writing grammatical sentences

page 65

1 **a** *The Simpsons* [has been running] for more than 10 years.
b Paper books [have] a future.
c Mobile phones [are being used] for many everyday purposes.
d Graffiti [has] a bad name.
e Most television cartoons [aim] only to entertain.
f Computer technology [is being updated] constantly.

2 Sample sentence corrections provided for non-sentences.
a NS. It has entertained people for a very long time
b S
c S
d NS. It was first shown on American television in 1990.
e S
f NS. It began in the subways of New York City.

3 **a** Video games can develop children's imagination, but they can also encourage violence. **OR** Video games can develop children's imagination. However, they can also encourage violence.
b Video games develop problem solving skills. Furthermore, they require considerable concentration.
c Everyone has a different view on art. Most people cannot be persuaded to change their minds. **OR** Everyone has a different view on art, and most people cannot be persuaded to change their minds.
d There are books for reading, and there are books for reference.
e Most cartoon shows are aimed at children. However, *The Simpsons* clearly targets adult viewers as well.
f Video games develop some very useful skills. For example, they improve reflexes.
g We can read books on computer screens, and/or we can read them in hand-held e-books.

h This show must be more than a comedy. Otherwise it would not be so popular.
i Children are playing computer games more and more, and watching TV less.
j Unfortunately most graffiti is ugly. Therefore it should not be legalised.

4 Sample sentence corrections provided for dependent clauses (DC)
a DC. Older people hate all graffiti, whereas young people think quite differently.
b S
c DC. Whenever you get on a train or bus or other form of public transport, you can see examples of graffiti.
d S
e S
f DC. We should be more open-minded about electronic books, because there are many reasons in favour of the new technology.

HELP! TASK

- A clause with only a part-verb is used as a sentence ie. *Making them more like a real book.*
- A phrase with no verb is used as a sentence ie. *Very annoying.*
- There are two places where two main clauses are linked with a comma, ie:

  For example, electronic books with soft covers would be a good idea, electronic books with something to turn the pages would be useful too. and,

  The other thing that would be needed would be a long-running battery, this would mean you would not be interrupted in the middle of an exciting story because of a flat battery.
- There is a dependent clause used as a sentence, ie: *Because people like the way books look and feel.*

Here is the paragraph with sentence structure errors corrected:
If electronic books could be made to be more like paper books, they may make books disappear. Because people like the way books look and feel, they are unlikely to rush to buy electronic books. For example, electronic books with soft covers would be a good idea. Electronic books with something to turn the pages would be useful too, because this would make them more like real books. The other thing that would be needed would be a long-running battery. This would mean you would not be interrupted in the middle of an exciting story because of a flat battery. Of course, this would be very annoying.

2 Using the right kind of language

page 70

1 **a** *Animal Farm* is an analogy for the Russian Revolution.
b The author, George Orwell, tried not to take sides even though he probably had his own beliefs and views.
c Robert Frost's strength lies in his use of symbolism.
d In both poems the symbolism was meaningful and full of moral value.
e His message seems to be that it is more rewarding to take the less common path when making an important life decision.

2 Sample answers:
a Even grandmothers and grandfathers have mobile phones.
b Many people lose their mobile phones and have to pay off their contracts.
c Many people prefer paper books because they have grown up with them.
d All members of the family can enjoy *The Simpsons*.
e Parents hate *The Simpsons* only because their children love it and want to watch it every night.

3 E-book manufacturers are betting that <u>changing consumer attitudes</u>, driven by the <u>explosion of Internet use</u> in recent years and <u>the ready acceptance of hand-held devices</u> ... have created <u>a new and sympathetic market</u>.

<u>The greatest obstacle to acceptance of any e-book</u> is <u>the "Can I take it bed with me?" syndrome</u>. Books – even the tackiest, well-read paperback – are <u>intimate, tactile objects</u> as well as <u>portable repositories for words, images and ideas</u>, and if an e-book doesn't have <u>an acceptable cuddle factor</u>, most people who read for pleasure will remain bound to <u>the analog version.</u>

4 **a** - **v**
b - **iii**
c - **i**
d - **iv**
e - **ii**

5 **a** <u>Aboriginal art</u> was used for <u>religious, social and educational purposes.</u>
b <u>Aboriginal art</u> has been acclaimed around the world for <u>its originality and design.</u>
c <u>The diet of Aboriginal groups</u> was greatly influenced by <u>their location.</u>
d <u>Survival</u> depended on <u>their knowledge of the seasonal availability of food and water.</u>
e <u>Rules of social behaviour</u> strongly influenced <u>intra-family relationships.</u>

6 **a** The population is expected to reach 22 million in the next few years.
b The word 'witchcraft' is used to refer to worship of the Devil.
c Witches were considered anti-Christian, amoral members of society.
d Biodiversity is measured as the number of species or subspecies of plants, animals and micro-organisms.
e Greek religion is thought to date from about the 2nd millennium BC.

HELP! TASK

- The writer refers to herself eg. *I have read, the other day on the radio I heard, we live in ...*
- She refers to individual people or groups eg. *the people in my suburb.*
- The writer needs to use fewer words, eg. take out *the other day on the radio I heard that ..., they would get people to ... and then when there was ... and different words*
- She could focus better on the processes, factors etc. by using nominalisations and the passive voice eg. changing *inventors are making mobile phones more and more advanced* to *mobile phones are becoming more and more advanced,* changing *They would get people to register their mobile numbers* to *Numbers would be placed on a register.*

One possible rewriting to make the language more appropriate for an essay is:

Mobile phones are becoming more and more advanced in terms of their communication capabilities. For example, trials are currently taking place of a system whereby mobile phones would be used to warn people about approaching bushfires and storms in their area. Numbers would be placed on a register and text messages sent in emergencies to all numbers on the register. This is an extremely useful application of mobile phone technology because of the large numbers of people in Australia in disaster-prone areas.

3 Referencing your work page 75

1 *Clean Up Australia Online* (online), www.cleanup.com.au, last updated 6th March 2002.

King, J. (2001) "Are we safe?" in *Science Today*, June, pp. 22 - 24.

Logan, J. & Todd, L. (2000) *Your local environment*, Hill End Publications, Melbourne.

Logan, J. & Todd, L. (2002) *Are our homes endangering our lives*? Blackman Publishing, Brisbane.

Looking into the future (video), 2002, Century 21 Films.

Roach, J. (2002) " Phone danger" in *The Western News*, Feb 16, p. 17.

Note: You could use underlining instead of italics.

3 Sample answers:

a As Xia Lin & Hubbard (online, 2000) have noted, the overall influence of e-Books on the environment remains unclear.

Xia Lin & Hubbard (online, 2000) discuss the effects of increasing electronic forms of publishing on paper use.

b Murphy (2001) reports on research which shows that people who have grown up with mobile phones tend to use their thumbs when others use their fingers.

It seems that mobile phones have led to an increasing use of our thumbs to do tasks once performed with our fingers (Murphy, 2001).

4 Using good spelling strategies page 79

1/3 Incorrect spelling is followed by correct spelling in brackets

wich (which); you'r (you're **or** your); dicides (decides) peopple (people); reveiw (review); sinse (since); devide (divide); actualy (actually); durring (during); allmost (almost)

2 nationality, independence, personally, deliberately, considerable, audience, interested, criticism, basically, activities, frightened, culture

4
a medicine
b sign
c benefit
d separately
e mixture
f racism
g citizen
h government

5
a believe
b receive
c thief
d receipt
e priest
f vein
g fierce
h neighbour
i achieve
j reign
k veil
l field

5 Getting the punctuation right page 82

1/2

a Henry VIII was the second son of Henry VII and Elizabeth of York. Henry was being educated for the church, but when his elder brother died, Henry became heir to the throne.

b Henry's reign began with much feasting and sport. After his father's solid rule, the energetic, youthful and handsome King avoided governing in person. He preferred to journey the countryside, hunting, and reviewing his subjects.

c The Celtic people were not a united people. Though they had a common culture, they were divided into tribes across various parts of Britain and Europe. Common traditions and language linked them. So too did a close similarity in laws.

d Though males generally dominated Celtic society, women had considerable freedom. For example, they could own their own property and even lead battles.

e As everyone had to farm for food, most Celts were farmers who could also be part-time warriors or noblemen. Artists and other learned people were very highly regarded and this demonstrates a highly civilised culture.

f Alexander the Great lived a hard and rough life, fighting battles and conquering land everywhere he went. He lived to be thirty three years of age. Had he lived longer, he may have conquered the whole world.

3
a Although its exact origins are lost in time, Greek religion is thought to date from about the 2nd millenium BC.

b The Greeks expected religion to explain natural phenomena, such as lightning, thunder and storms at sea.

c The ancient Greeks believed that temples were a place for gods to visit, not, as it sometimes thought, a place of worship.

d Our earliest surviving examples of Greek literature are *The Iliad* and *The Odyssey*, which record men's interactions with various gods and goddesses.

e Greeks believed that gods often spoke through oracles, such as the Oracle of Apollo at Delphi, in order to help humans understand the wishes of the gods.

f Before about 600BC, the statues, whether made of wood or stone, seem to have been relatively small.

4
a Its
b It's
c its
d its
e It's

5
a Apostrophe not needed – forests simply a plural form, no possession indicated.
b Apostrophe not needed.
c planet's – apostrophe needed to show that *planet* (singular) 'owns' *survival* (ie. the survival of our planet).
d Australia's - apostrophe needed to show that *Australia* owns *population.*
e No apostrophe needed.
f Scientists' – apostrophe needed to show that *scientists* (plural) own *concerns.*
g Politicians' – apostrophe need to show *politicians* (plural) own *views.*
h No apostrophe needed.